Adolescents in Crisis

Adolescents in Crisis offers a psychoanalytic perspective on the difficulties that can arise when young people renegotiate their relationship with the world and their own bodies as they experience puberty.

This edited collection explores the tension adolescents often experience between their wish to develop and grow up, alongside the concurrent urge to regress towards a pre-pubescent way of relating to their own self and others. Covering the period from pre-teen years to the dawn of adulthood, and including clinical vignettes throughout, the contributors look at issues such as isolation, self-harm, eating disorders, gender identity and delinquent behaviors. These are often used as defense strategies against feelings of powerlessness and inadequacy that puberty can trigger. Each chapter draws on traditional and contemporary psychoanalytic thought to help the reader understand these anxieties and provide guidance on how the therapist, parent and adolescent can work through them together, allowing the young person to explore new ways of managing their anxieties.

Part of the 101 Kids books series, this book is an invaluable resource for psychoanalysts and psychotherapists working with young people, as well as teachers, social workers and parents dealing with adolescents in difficulty.

Emanuela Quagliata is a Training and Supervising Psychoanalyst working in private practice in Rome, Italy. She teaches at the Tavistock-model trainings in Florence and at the Institute of Psychoanalysis in Rome, she is Chair for Europe of the IPA Committee on Women and Psychoanalysis. Emanuela is the author of *Becoming Parents and Overcoming Obstacles* (2013) and, with Margaret Rustin, she is the editor of *Assessment in Child Psychotherapy* (2000).

Alessandra Marsoni is a London based Adolescent and Adult Psychotherapist working in private practice with children, adolescents, parents and adult patients. She worked in the Adolescent Department at the Tavistock Clinic in London where until recently she ran the Adolescent Workshop for the Child Psychotherapy training.

101 Kids
Series Editor: Emanuela Quagliata

101 Kids, a collection created and directed by Emanuela Quagliata, a psychoanalyst and specialist in working with children, adolescents, and families, is intended for parents but also for professionals working with children, ranging from psychotherapists, paediatricians, teachers, nurses, etc.

The series contains 6 single-subject volumes, each dedicated to the key stages which mark the life of children, from pregnancy to adolescence. The underlying thinking of the series is psychoanalytic, but it is made accessible to a wider, not only specialistic, audience. The authors, some of whom are leading worldwide experts in their respective fields, attempt to offer parents a new point of view, from which to observe their relationship with their own children. This will help them understand the meaning of various forms of behaviour, as well as the fears and conflicts faced by children and adolescents.

Adolescents in Crisis: A Psychoanalytic Approach to the Challenges of Adolescence
Edited by Emanuela Quagliata and Alessandra Marsoni

For more information about this series, please visit: www https://www.routledge.com/

Adolescents in Crisis

A Psychoanalytic Approach to the
Challenges of Adolescence

Edited by Emanuela Quagliata and
Alessandra Marsoni

Routledge
Taylor & Francis Group

LONDON AND NEW YORK

Designed cover image: Algy Craig Hall

First published 2026
by Routledge
4 Park Square, Milton Park, Abingdon, Oxon OX14 4RN

and by Routledge
605 Third Avenue, New York, NY 10158

Routledge is an imprint of the Taylor & Francis Group, an informa business

British Library Cataloguing-in-Publication Data
A catalogue record for this book is available from the British Library

ISBN: 978-1-032-39749-8 (hbk)
ISBN: 978-1-032-39747-4 (pbk)
ISBN: 978-1-003-35118-4 (ebk)

DOI: 10.4324/9781003351184

Typeset in Times New Roman
by Newgen Publishing UK

This book is dedicated to Margot Waddell whose profound understanding of adolescence has inspired and helped us as well as so many young patients, parents and clinicians.

Contents

Contributors

The Authors

FRANCO D'ALBERTON is a psychologist, psychotherapist and psychoanalysts, he is a member of the Italian Psychoanalytic Society (SPI) and of the Societé Européenne del l'Enfant et de l'Adolescence (Sepea). He worked extensively in paediatric settings, such as the Paediatric Department at the S. Orsola Hospital in Bologna. His publications include: *Psychoanalytic Work with Children in Hospital (2022), Children Exposed to Pornographic Images on the Internet: General and Specific Aspects in a Psychoanalytic Perspective,* (2021).

ROBIN ANDERSON is a Consultant Child and Adolescent Psychiatrist, a Training Analyst and a Supervisor at the British Psychoanalytical Society. Until 2000, he was the Chair of the Adolescent Department at the Tavistock Clinic in London. During this period, his research and clinical practice focused on suicide and self-harming behaviours. He has published numerous studies in psychoanalysis and psychotherapy, addressing childhood, adolescence, and adulthood, with a particular interest in the emergence of early object relations during adolescence, especially in the work with young people at risk of suicide. He is the author of many articles, he curated the volumes *Clinical Lectures on Klein and Bion*, and he coedited, with Anna Dartington, *Facing It Out: Clinical Perspectives on Adolescent Disturbance.*

DONALD CAMPBELL is a Training Analyst and a Supervisor. He was the President of the British Psychoanalytical Society and the General Secretary of the International Psychoanalytical Association (IPA). For thirty years, he worked at the Portman Clinic in London, providing psychoanalytic psychotherapy to children, adolescents, and adults exhibiting violent, antisocial behaviours or struggling with perversions. He has published extensively on adolescence, suicide, violence, childhood sexual abuse, and perversion. From 1976 to 1989, he collaborated at the Brent Consultation Centre established by Moses and Eglé Laufer. Alongside Rob Hale, he published *Working in the Dark: Understanding the Pre-Suicide State of Mind* in 2017. Campbell has always been open to different ideas and schools of thought. In 2020, he edited a book with Ronny Jaffe

When the Body Speaks: a British-Italian Dialogue. The book is a collection of papers, written by analysts with diverse theoretical backgrounds, on topics related to the mind and the body.

Eglé LAUFER (1925–2021) was the President of the Brent Centre for Young People, which she co-founded in 1967 with her husband Moses Laufer, alongside Mervin Glasser, Maurice Friedman, and Myer Wohl. It was the first psychoanalytically oriented centre in the United Kingdom dedicated specifically to adolescents. Laufer and her husband formed a professional partnership that established them as pioneers in adolescent psychoanalysis. A supervising analyst, a Distinguished Fellow of the British Psychoanalytical Society, she co-founded the Adolescence Forum within the European Federation of Psychoanalysis. Among her most significant publications are the articles *Some Prerequisites for Psychoanalytic Work with Adolescents* and *Adolescence: Before and Beyond Breakdown*, as well as the seminal volume *Adolescence and Developmental Breakdown*, co-authored with Moses Laufer in 1984, which contains some of their most influential theoretical contributions.

ALESSANDRA LEMMA is a Fellow of the British Psychoanalytic Society and a Chartered Clinical and Counselling Psychologist. She is a Visiting Professor in the Psychoanalysis Unit, University College London and Consultant, Clinical Psychologist Anna Freud Centre. For 16 years she worked at the Tavistock Clinic where she was, at different stages, Head of Psychology and Professor of Psychological Therapies in conjunction with Essex University. She was a recipient of the 2022 Sigourney Award in recognition of her theoretical and clinical contributions to understanding body modification practices, the impacts of technology on psychic functioning and transgender identities, as well as for her efforts in developing and disseminating worldwide a brief psychoanalytic intervention for mood disorders. She is the former General Editor of the New Library of Psychoanalysis book series and is the current Chair of the International Journal of Psychoanalysis' Management Board. Her most recent books are: *Transgender Identities: A Contemporary Introduction* (Routledge, 2021 and Franco Angeli, 2022), *First Principles: Applied Ethics for Psychoanalytic Practice* (OUP, 2023) and *Introduction to the Practice of Psychoanalytic Therapy – Third Edition* (Wiley, 2025).

ALESSANDRA MARSONI is a child, adolescent and adult psychotherapist trained at the Tavistock Clinic and at the British Psychotherapy Foundation. She has an extensive background in mental health settings within the NHS. She worked in the eating disorders team at Great Ormond Street Hospital and in the Child and Adolescent Mental Health Service (CAMHS) at St Ann's and North Middlesex Hospitals. She has a special interest in adolescent mental health problems, having worked in the Adolescent Department at the Tavistock Clinic in London for over ten years. She has worked with a variety of adolescent pathologies, ranging from depression, eating disorders, deliberate self-harm, anxieties and compulsive behaviours. For many years she had a teaching role at the Tavistock Clinic where she ran a weekly workshop on adolescents for the Child Psychotherapy training. She is now full-time in private practice where she sees children, adolescents, parents, as well as adult patients.

ROBERTA MONDADORI is a Consultant Child and Adolescent Psychotherapist. She studied and qualified at the Tavistock Clinic in London. In 1998, she completed a Master's degree in Psychoanalytic Psychotherapy from the University of East London. She has taught on various Tavistock-model courses in both England and Italy. For many years, she taught the postgraduate course on eating disorders offered jointly by the Tavistock Clinic and the University of East London, in both London and Bologna. Currently, she works in private practice and teaches at the Tavistock Clinic and at the Martha Harris Study Centre in Florence. She is the author of several articles published in the Journal of Child Psychotherapy and the International Journal of Infant Observation. She has also contributed to the volumes *Exploring Eating Disorders in Adolescents: The Generosity of Acceptance*, edited by G. Williams (2004), and *The Handbook of Child and Adolescent Psychotherapy*, edited by M. Lanyado and A. Horne (2009).

JACK NOVICK and KERRY KELLY NOVICK are training and supervising analysts of the American Psychoanalytic Association, the International Psychoanalytic Association (IPA) and the Contemporary Freudian Society. They work with children, adolescents and adults. They trained with Anna Freud in London, and they have always combined clinical practice with teaching and research. They are the founders of the Allen Creek Preschool in Ann Arbor. Since the 1960s, the Novicks have collaborated on numerous volumes and authored many articles published in leading psychoanalytic journals. Their works include *Working with Parents* (2005) and *Emotional Muscle: Strong Parents, Strong Children* (2010), the latter is currently used as a textbook in psychoanalytic training courses.

EMANUELA QUAGLIATA is a Training and supervising psychoanalyst of the Italian Psychoanalytical Society (SPI) and the International Psychoanalytic Association (IPA). She has a doctorate in recurrent miscarriage and infertility. She teaches in various training programs based on the Tavistock model and at the National Training Institute of the SPI. A member of the IPA's Child and Adolescent Psychoanalysis Committee, she is both co-author and editor of several volumes published by the Italian publisher Astrolabio, these include: *Neonati visti da vicino* (1993), *Un buon incontro* (1994), which focuses on assessment in the developmental age, and *Un bisogno vitale* (2002), which explores eating disorders in children and adolescents. In 2018, she published *Becoming Parents and Overcoming Obstacles*, on the complex themes of postnatal depression, infertility, miscarriage and premature births. She has edited a series of books for parents '101kids' published by Astrolabio.

JUDE PIERCEY is a psychoanalytic psychotherapist and clinical supervisor in private practice in Sydney. She works with adults, children, adolescents and parents and teaches Infant Observation at The Institute of Child and Adolescent Psychoanalytic Psychotherapy (ICAPP). Her work has been presented and published internationally.

JENNY SPRINCE is a Consultant Child and Adolescent Psychotherapist, trained at the Tavistock Clinic in London. She is the Clinical Director at Placement Support, a specialist provider of therapeutic services for looked after children and their carers She is the Chair of Management Committee at APPCIOS (The association of Psychodynamic Practice and Counselling in Organisational Settings). She has published extensively on adoption and trauma.

GIANNA WILLIAMS is a Consultant Child, Adolescent and Adult Psychoanalyst, she is a member of the British Psychoanalytical Society. As a Consultant Child and Adolescent Psychotherapist at the Tavistock Clinic, she played a pivotal role in introducing the Tavistock Model to five Italian cities. She included Infant Observation seminars in the training for Child Neuropsychiatry at the University of Pisa. Since 1999, she has served as a Consultant for the non-has been doing consultation work for the governmental organization "Juntos con los Niños," dedicated to supporting street children in Mexico. Williams has published extensively and contributed to numerous volumes, with a particular focus on eating disorders. Her notable works include *Internal Landscapes and Foreign Bodies: Eating Disorders and Other Pathologies* (1997). She also edited the 2004 volume *The Generosity of Acceptance.*

Introduction

'When a caterpillar is about to become a butterfly, it goes through a truly difficult time.' With these words, a grandmother attempts to console her sixteen-year-old granddaughter, who is going through a profound crisis during puberty.

In the period which spans from the beginning through to the end of secondary school (though today, this process extends well beyond the secondary school years), adolescents undergo a profound process of renegotiation and revaluation of their sense of self. This generates in them significant tension between the desire for change and the opposing force to hold on to their previous way of relating to themselves and to others. The grandmother's metaphor encapsulates the inevitable changes that occur during puberty: the world is no longer what it once was, and it will never be the same again. The body changes in shape, strength and size; the voice alters, and for girls, the development of breasts marks the attainment of sexual maturity. Adolescents also experience significant social and emotional changes. Relationships with peers become more intimate, they experiment with new sexual relationships, there is a difficult transition from dependence on the parents to interdependence with others. Ultimately, this process leads to couple relationships and parenting capabilities, which involve greater autonomy and responsibility in making important life decisions.

The biological changes, accompanied by intense emotions and fantasies about the self and the body, provoke a sense of dislocation and loss, something which Anna Freud compared to the process of mourning. The complexity of these physical and emotional changes triggers anxieties, concerns, often serious crises, which adolescents try to manage by activating defences against feelings of helplessness and inadequacy. These defences are sometimes based on omnipotent fantasies that can become rather terrifying when the newly acquired physical capabilities actually allow adolescents to act on what so far were 'only' phantasies.

This volume addresses the meaning of these crises, the choice of defensive manoeuvres, and their impact on adolescents, their parents, and the adults surrounding them.

Since no aspect of life remains unchanged during this period, a certain degree of internal and external stability is necessary to avoid being overwhelmed by anxiety and a sense of helplessness. The strength and stability needed to face change are

DOI: 10.4324/9781003351184-1

rooted in the introjection of benevolent parental figures, in positive dependency on adults, trust in them, and an adequate understanding of one's emotions. In the absence of these experiences, adolescents may choose certain defence mechanisms in order to manage anxiety. This is particularly the case when young people find themselves in a hostile external world and are in a state of emotional alert in the face of a present or future 'danger.'

A symptom, a state of extreme isolation, an act of self-harm, antisocial or delinquent acting-out behaviour, aim at maintaining a relative sense of security. Although these behaviours are maladaptive in the external world, they may represent the best solution adolescents can negotiate, given the external circumstances and their internal resources. When we think about a self-destructive mental state, we have in mind not only actions (such as anorexia, substance abuse, violence, self-harm, or suicide attempts), but also aspects of the personality that undermine relationships, growth, and development, thus destroying any possibility of intimacy. These defensive strategies may be effective for a limited period of time and in specific situations. When an adolescent seeks help from a psychotherapist, it is evident that their system of defences for managing internal turbulence has failed. Seeing a therapist may be experienced as a potential rescue, approached with suspicion or perhaps indifference. This reaction provides us with an insight into the adolescent's internal capacity to reflect on their experiences and to utilize the help that is offered. This capacity is often closely linked to the quality of the internalized parental figures, who may or may not be related to their relationship with real parents, either present or past.

What unites young children and adolescents is the intensity of emotions that those who are close to them have to bear. Being at the receiving end of painful projections makes it difficult, at times, to be the parent of a young person. Often parents are, on the one hand burdened with unwanted feelings of fear, incompetence, and despair, on the other, whilst managing this emotional barrage, they also need to hold on to the capacity to bear the concerns for their son/daughter. Parents must take responsibility for the situation and make important decisions, even if they might feel powerless and without hope.

The purpose of this book is to help parents realize that when an adolescent in crisis starts to act in a self-destructive or antisocial way, these behaviours are 'protective': they are meant to provide a solution to emotional and mental conflicts that are too difficult to negotiate.

In the first chapter, Alessandra Marsoni sets the scene by providing some key facts on adolescent development with its different tasks and challenges. The chapter focuses on the struggle of identity formation, that is, the psychological work that gradually enables us to find a new sense of self, different from our parents and yet deeply connected to them. It is a balancing act, one which implies big losses – first of all, of the child's identity with its safety, under the protection/influence of the parents – but there is also an exciting sense of growth. How does the young person acquire a 'mind of one's own', as opposed to acquired, 'pseudo' identities or an identity which is still very much defined by parents and family? How does one find a sense of self which is an evolution, not a replica of the one passed down by the parents?

In the second chapter, Jenny Sprince expands on the theme of identity and focuses on the process of separation and individuation. She starts from a very early phase of development, when mother and baby are entirely fused on one another, in a state of 'twinship'. In this phase there is no differentiation, the breast of the mother is 'an all providing cornucopia', the baby is immersed in the world of the mother. At this early stage the father is almost redundant to the mother/baby dyad. Sprince highlights how these early experiences affect a preconception of gender and gender specific body parts. The baby gradually separates from the mother and starts to include 'otherness', the father and other family members. The anxiety of puberty reactivates and often exacerbates these primitive gender polarizations. The adolescent is pulled back towards a fusion/twinship, this time with others, as the baby did with the mother.

The turmoil, physical and emotional, brought by puberty is at the centre of Franco D'Alberton's chapter, the third one. Changes in the body (height and size suddenly shoot up as well as sexual hormones which were very low during childhood), in the functioning of the brain, precede psychological maturity and this gap is hard to negotiate, for young people and their parents. Puberty tears the young person apart from the world of childhood, its safety and all the connections with the world of the parents. D'Alberton focuses on his work with children who present with physical symptoms which had been thoroughly investigated by paediatricians; however, no organic cause could 'explain' the symptomatology. D'Alberton's task is to assess a possible emotional problem underlying the physical complaint. Interestingly, the requests are mostly related to secondary school children or to young children. These are indeed the two major periods in which the body lends itself to expressing psychological dynamics.

In the fourth chapter, Alessandra Lemma focuses on the experience of being an adolescent in a digital world, a world that the adults around them – parents, teachers, therapists – did not experience. The emotional and physical pressure that comes from the changing, messy pubertal body can be mitigated by an immersion in the virtual world, from gaming, social media to online pornography. The experience of being-in-a-body can be bypassed, the real body avoided and transformed, redesigned into a virtual one. This 'onlife' existence can be used as a refuge against the challenges of being a real adolescent in a real body.

Jude Piercey's chapter, the fifth one, deals with the difficulties of parenting an adolescent. Parents often describe a sense of shock when faced with the rapid changes, physical and emotional, that flood their son/daughter and themselves. It is a bit like swimming from the shallow to the deep end of a pool. What Jude Piercey defines as 'collaborative parent work' is a well-researched therapeutic approach which aims at integrating, rather than separation, work with parents and with the adolescent patient. The parents are met regularly, in parallel to the therapy of the young person, by the same therapist who sees their son/daughter. Jude Piercey illustrates this method of collaborative work with interesting extracts from sessions with a set of parents and sessions with their daughter.

In the following chapter, Kerry Kelly Novick and Jack Novick propose a similar model of intervention in which the same therapist sees the adolescent and also offers regular appointments to the parents. The idea of involving the parents in this way doesn't hinder individual work with the adolescent but, on the contrary, it strengthens and makes it more effective. Of course, not all therapeutic interventions can or should be identical, and the authors do not intend to establish rules for involving parents. Sometimes adolescents reject the idea of their psychotherapist meeting their parents. In other cases, parents are unwilling to be involved, and often it is more appropriate for them to work with a different clinician. What is important is that the therapist holds the parents very much in mind and at the same time that the adolescent is reassured that the confidentiality of the therapeutic relationship will be respected.

Conflicts underlying body-related disorders, such as eating disorders or body image disturbances, are often rooted in narcissistic issues and difficulties in accepting dependence on others. Gianna Williams and Roberta Mondadori, in the seventh chapter, describe the development of a narcissistic disorder. This involves turning to parts of the self that offer a false protection from mental pain and at the same time deny the presence of an internal needy part, that does depend on external sources of help and support. In this way, the anorexic patient wants to avoid a dependency on food and suppresses the feeling of hunger. The chapter addresses the increasingly common problem of anorexia and bulimia, focusing on different developmental stages (from children to adolescents) and different levels of severity.

In the eighth chapter, Robin Anderson touches on the difficult theme of violence against the self, whether through self-harm or suicidal acts. He emphasizes the importance of careful risk assessment, alongside a deep understanding of the patient's mental state. Suicidal fantasies are common in adolescence: sometimes they are fleeting and might not lead to serious risk. However, adolescents who constantly ruminate on such ideas are likely to be depressed and they are seriously at risk of attempting suicide. The author describes various motivations behind such attempts: the desire to kill an intolerable part of the self, to eliminate a destructive internal object, or to escape from persecutors. Choosing suicide may represent a drastic and dramatic solution to a psychological problem. This is achieved through the projection, the concrete elimination, through death, of an emotional experience that cannot be shared or processed.

In relation to the violence of emotions, Donald Campbell examines, in the ninth chapter, aggression and antisocial behaviour, which affect both the victim and the figures of authority, starting with the parents. These risky and often violent behaviours provide an 'alternative' to the challenges of growing up. The question is, how do parents assess the severity of these actions and the risk of their recurrence? It is not uncommon for them to feel shame or guilt for their child's antisocial behaviour. In order to avoid these unpleasant feelings, parents either try to minimize the problems, ignore them, or act in a persecutory and punitive way, which usually makes things worse.

Emanuela Quagliata in conversation with Eglé Laufer in the last years of her life, explains and reviews the concept of 'developmental breakdown,' the crisis that leads to an interruption in developmental processes. Alongside feelings of abandonment of previous certainties, some adolescents can be overwhelmed by the experience of losing control of their body (often by feeling that they are losing their mind) and of their earlier, more predictable, identity. This juncture can easily precipitate a crisis which might result in a developmental breakdown. Dissatisfaction with or rejection of oneself can lead to self-loathing and self-harm. There is the risk that an interest and care for one's body becomes excessive, potentially leading to obsessive behaviours and eating disorders. Apathy can lead to isolation and dangerous dependencies, especially if the adolescent's difficulties stem, in part, from family dynamics.

This volume could also be titled 'Adolescents and Parents in Crisis,' as the phases of distress and pain adolescents go through profoundly affect their parents' emotional states and the balance of the entire family. Some parents desperately try to avoid their adolescent's difficulties and anxieties: this usually represents a defensive strategy to maintain an apparent 'harmony'. This attitude that we sometimes see in parents often reinforces the young person's sense of isolation, it might even trigger in the adolescent a further denial of the need to rely on the parents. However, dealing with a young person who is withdrawn, hostile, or engaged in self-harming behaviours poses many challenges, not only to the parents but also to the therapist. An environment (parents, family, school) which can tolerate the rapid, at times dramatic changes that might occur in the life of the adolescent, is crucial. At the same time, it is important that the adults involved are willing and able to provide firm support to the ongoing therapeutic work. For this reason, while individual therapy remains the primary space where growth and change occur for the adolescent, it can be extremely helpful to work with the parents in parallel, in order to support and facilitate the therapy of the young person.

Beyond the challenges that may arise in individual psychotherapies, it is essential for the therapist to always have in mind the parent-child relationship, seen from the different aspects of the therapeutic intervention. This volume wants to facilitate a reflection, from a psychoanalytic perspective, on these moments of crisis; the aim is to help parents and children, as well as therapists and teachers, make sense of and navigate the complex experiences which are so much at the core of adolescence.

Emanuela Quagliata and Alessandra Marsoni

Chapter 1

Identity formation in adolescence

Alessandra Marsoni

Introduction

There are several angles we can take to think about identity formation. These different approaches to identity are all interesting and important in their own right. There is a social identity and a cultural one, both rooted in society and culture (Ferrer-Wreder, Kroger, 2020). There is also sexual identity and gender identity; there is an identity which is greatly influenced by social privileges, discrimination, and structural inequalities. This is what is referred to as identity intersectionality, that is, 'the total package of how people put together their identity in combination with what society deems as important'. (Ferrer-Wreder, Kroeger, p. 158)

As the crucial work on identity begins in adolescence, let me give you a brief overview on this important and challenging period of our lives.

Adolescent development: some key facts

It is now a common belief that adolescence is a crucial phase in human life, a period of intense growth and significant changes. This has not always been the case: in the 70's adolescence was considered a rather neat 'age between' childhood and adulthood (Miller, 1998); a passing stage, full of turbulence and adjustments that, it was then believed, time would heal, regardless of intervention or treatment.

We now know that intervention is in fact, very important and can prevent mental illnesses in adulthood. If problems that arise in adolescence are left untreated, they can persist and become accentuated in adulthood. Furthermore, what is now considered 'adolescence' is a longer period, between the ages of 12 (or whenever the onset of puberty occurs) and 24. It might be worth mentioning that the Adolescent Department at the Tavistock Clinic in London, one of Britain's centres of expertise on adolescence, does take referrals of 'adolescent' patients up to the age of 25.

The now accepted, although a bit artificial, view is that adolescence is divided into three periods:

DOI: 10.4324/9781003351184-2

First Adolescence: (11–15 years)

These are the years of puberty which bring tremendous and sudden changes to the body. This is a unique event in the course of a life; only the foetus in the uterus undergoes a greater rate of physical changes, a phenomenon that doesn't happen again after birth. Various authors in this book highlight the maelstrom, both physical and emotional, brought about by the onset of puberty. A few years ago, a patient of mine, Maya, described her shock and horror when she looked at her naked body in the mirror,' I could not believe it, I had turned into my mother!'. Maya always had a bad relationship with her mother, even as a child. Puberty had turned the body of a child into the body of a woman, in Maya's mind, that of her mother. These physical changes triggered an emotional turmoil in Maya, who felt invaded from within by a mother she had always tried to keep at bay.

Physiological, endocrinological, neurological changes take place, sometimes, especially in girls, before emotional ones. Substantial bodily changes – menstruation, production of semen/ejaculation, appearance of bodily hair, breaking of the voice – bring chaos to a young person's identity, the self as it has been known so far. This physical and emotional upheaval propels the young person into a totally new world, one in which parents no longer occupy their usual, safe, place in the adolescent's mind. It is the beginning of the difficult process of disentangling one's identity from the parental one.

Middle Adolescence (15–18 years)

The process of identity individuation continues. More challenges are on the way: the stresses of school, peer pressure, the importance of friendships and a new challenge: how does the developing young person dislodge the parents from the throne the child had given them?

Late Adolescence (18–21 years)

This is another difficult time, although in different ways: it marks the end of the school years, university life now within reach, and adult life just round the corner – a challenging prospect that can easily provoke anxiety and potentially trigger an array of distinctive crises.

The challenges that the young person has to face over these years are substantial: some people manage them relatively easily, others find them hard but they get through. Yet for some young people, the changes and challenges brought by the delicate transition from childhood to adolescence, via the upheaval of puberty, can be overwhelming. As Margot Waddell reminds us in her beautiful book *On Adolescence*, 'at any age transition suggests instability, loss, change, uncertainty, the unknown' I would leave quotation marks, it is a quote from MW's book. (Waddell, 2018, p. 46). If this transition is felt to be unmanageable then adolescent development, with its ordinary flow of ups and downs, becomes an impossible hurdle; first of all for the young person involved but also, for parents who have to navigate unchartered territories – especially if it is their first experience of an adolescent in the family. Jude Pierce in her chapter, uses an evocative analogy to describe the parents, feeling out of their depth when confronted with an adolescent: it is like swimming from the shallow to the deep end of a pool.

In the different chapters of this book, the authors tackle some of the most common defensive mechanisms young people resort to in order to protect themselves from feeling too overwhelmed by the changes and challenges they have to face. Such a defence could be provided by a refuge in the safety of the virtual world; in other cases it could be a withdrawal in an eating disorder, or in self-harm or, in extreme cases, in suicidal thinking; I would substitute das with semicolon in all these scenarios the young person doesn't have to deal with the 'instability, loss, change and uncertainty' brought by the difficult transition into adolescence.

Identity as 'A mind of one's own'

My chapter will focus on yet another challenge, one which, in my clinical experience with young people and their parents, seems to run as a common thread. It is the process of letting go of the identity of our childhood, which was very much modelled on our parents, in order to establish what will eventually be an adult identity. This process includes and at the same time excludes our parents: it is a real balancing act, a lifelong enterprise which begins in adolescence. At birth, our body separates from the body of our mother, but it takes much longer to separate psychologically.

This separation is a central and difficult task for young people, it is the beginning of a gradual 'finding a mind of one's own', echoing Virginia Woolf's room of one's own. As Margot Waddell wonders in the above-mentioned book,'how does a person's internal room become structured and furnished in its unique and idiosyncratic way – not as a prefab, identikit, design-catalogue sort of room but as a space of one's own?' (Waddell, 2018, p. 133). We could add to the metaphor that the 'pre-fab' kind of room/space is one that comes straight from the parents, it is their 'model'.

Peter Blos, who, with Erik Erikson, is one of the first psychoanalysts to enquire seriously into the phenomenon of identity formation in adolescence, talks about the 'second individuation process' (Blos, 1967). It is the delicate moment when the young person lets go of the parental figures, internalised over the childhood years and at the core of one's identity. Blos explains that there is a first individuation process, ending with the third year of life. In this process the child leaves the symbiosis with the mother and gradually gains some independence from the maternal presence – through motor, verbal and cognitive advances – as well as through some degree of psychological separateness from the mother.

What is relevant for us clinicians working with adolescents, and for the parents of adolescents, is to bear in mind that there are important similarities between the first and the second process of individuation. Time and time again, in my work with parents, I can see their utter shock when faced with their adolescent who acts, or appears to act, like a child again, 'a huge toddler that we can't control!' this is a quote, why not quotation marks?, as a father said to me recently.

The mother of a 15-year-old boy described to me, with disbelief, the moment in which her son, when asked to switch off his phone at 10 pm, pushed her with such force that she almost fell down the stairs – they were both quite horrified by what had happened. Emotions, in such situations, can be sky high, as they can be in a toddler. But what was harmless in the past can now be lethal, – what was a gentle push can now become a fatal fall. It takes time to adjust to this change, both for the adults and for the young person. I see this difficulty very often in my work with parents. It can be extremely difficult for them to switch from having a defiant, moody, rebellious, reckless, extremely annoying, scary, frustrating… (just to pick some adjectives that capture many of the feelings involved) son or daughter who can quickly and unexpectedly turn into a fragile, child-like person. Parents can thus be faced with powerful emotions in themselves: a sense of helplessness as well as inadequacy, sadness for the child they have now lost. A tempestuous relationship with a young person might bring to the surface unexplored feelings of their relationship with their own parents, along with memories of their own adolescence. All this is complicated to manage whilst also managing a son or daughter in turmoil or, even worse, in crisis.

The similarities between these two different stages of development (the toddler stage and the adolescent one) are interesting and again it is worth having them in mind when we are confused and exasperated by an adolescent who behaves like a young child. Both periods have in common a heightened impulsivity (remember all the risky situations in which the toddler and later the adolescent can put him/herself…), together with a tremendous push towards independence, a desire to grow up, which is regularly followed by a regression into more dependency and a longing to remain a child. Both processes require two difficult but necessary challenges, that of separation and individuation. In the earlier process, individuation is a walking, talking toddler who can begin to let go of the physical presence of the mother: in the later one, individuation as a young person who is beginning to find a place outside the cocoon of the family. Blos reminds us that if these processes 'miscarry, they are followed by a specific deviant development that embodies the respective failure of individuation.' (Blos, 1967, p. 163). This can be problematic and in some extreme cases it may lead to psychopathology. I see the impact of these failures in some of my clinical work with adult patients who are still struggling to establish an identity properly separate from the parental one.

Let's have a closer look at the complexities of the separation/individuation process. With adolescence, we see the beginning of the shedding of family dependencies, the loosening of infantile ties that, with time, will enable the young person to become 'a member of the adult world' (Blos, 1967, p. 163). One of my patients, a 17-year-old boy, gradually became very cross with his mother who kept buying theatre tickets for him, as she used to do when he was a child – the booking was done without consulting him. At first, he accepted this imposition and he felt the rage silently. With time, he was able to rebel against his mother's decision, 'I want to decide what plays I want to see, I am not an 8-year-old anymore!'. He was extremely pleased with himself when his mother listened to him and allowed him to choose what interested him in the outside world – for this young person choosing his own interests, the plays he wanted to see, was the first step towards separating from his mother and becoming increasingly more aware of what his own interests were.

Another classic example is when the young person's identity is developed enough to openly contrast the parents' views of the world (for example, their political ideas or their values) and to express his/her own. This can bring fierce conflicts between the young person and the parents, but these conflicts are a necessary and helpful stage in the process of individuation.

Blos emphasises how important it is that 'new extra familial objects are sought outside the family, in the world (it could be school, experiences with new friends, role models in music, politics, theatre and so forth). I would add that it is equally important that the parents facilitate, rather than obstruct, this process. I often come across this problem in my clinical work: sometimes I see it from the point of view of the young person who struggles to let go of the familiar objects and become curious about new ones. Or in other cases, it is the opposite difficulty: the young person is keen to explore the world outside the family, the struggle this time is with the parents who don't want to lose the young version of their son/daughter, who is still very much under their influence and protection. This moment is also challenging for parents: it can be hard for them to feel that they are no longer the unchallenged 'Gods' in their child's universe. I come across parents, usually parents of 13-14 year olds, who struggle to 'allow' their child to grow up, they cling on to the child and resist the emerging adolescent.

During the pandemic, I worked with a mother who categorically refused her 14-year-old daughter to have any social media. As for long periods of time, during the two lockdowns, there was only online schooling, or intermittent in person attendance, this meant that the girl was totally isolated from her friends. The mother also insisted that her daughter go to bed at 9 pm, her nine year old brother's bed-time. It took some work in the sessions to help the mother realize that she was fighting her daughter's inevitable and healthy process of separating from her, of growing up, from childhood to early adulthood.

It is also important to observe how the shedding of the parental identity is done: it can be a violent rupture from childhood, an absolute rejection of the parents/families' values, a refusal of parental rules in favour of risky, rebellious, impulsive actions. Of course these behaviours are very common with adolescents; for many of them these are moments of respite from the parental authority and control, or exploration, of boundary testing but they are temporary, they pass; yet for others the sense of apparent liberation from the parents, their being at war with them, becomes enduring part of their identity and far more problematic.

In fact, an extreme turning away from the parents implies a failure of the delicate balance between separation and individuation, and is more of a manic circumvention of the delicate process of disengaging from the parents. As Blos explains, 'the incapacity to separate from internal objects except by detachment, rejection and debasement is subjectively experienced as alienation.' (Blos, 1967, p. 167)

Acquired identities

In my practice, the majority of my clinical work is with young people, although I also work with parents (the adolescent is seen by a colleague) and with adult patients. The combination of adolescent, parent and adult work, allows me to have a short- term as well as a long-term view on difficulties, more specifically, to our theme, the ones related to identity formation. I see them in action, from the point of view of the young person. I appreciate their impact on the parents and, last but not least, my adult work enables me to have a glance at what might happen in the future, if these difficulties are not resolved at the right developmental moment.

In the previous section, I tried to show how hard it is to 'become a subject', or to reach, by the end of adolescence, a sense of 'who I' am. I will now try to highlight some current 'stumbling blocks' on the path towards identity formation – this is a caveat for parents but it can also be helpful to clinicians working with adolescents.

Given the complexity of the separation/individuation process, many young people 'circumvent' this hurdle and try to acquire a ready formed identity, often this identity is greatly influenced by the parents or, in more entrenched cases, even imposed by them. This is a recurrent clinical presentation, one which, with some appropriate work, it is possible to shift, thus allowing the young person to find 'a room of his/her own'.

I often come across young people whose identity is completely 'handed down' not only by their parents but, in some cases, even by the previous generations, by the grandparents. Together with this form of identity often come high expectations to follow a path of achievements and success, one which, deep down, under the surface, might not at all fit the young person. This 'package', Margot Waddell's 'pre-fab, catalogue room', has become the identity of the family, close and extended: parents, siblings, cousins, they all share it, the young person has no choice but to acquire it. This can work for a while until something goes wrong and there is a crisis.

This is what happened to an 18-year-old, whom I shall call Andrew, who was referred to me after he failed his entry exam at a top university, the one his parents, siblings and grandparents attended. This rejection triggered a serious crisis in Andrew, he referred to it as a 'collapse': he felt lost, a disappointment to his family, unable to move forward in life. He had to take a year off – in his certainty to go to the top university he did not apply to another one, he did not have a plan B, and had to wait a year. These were hard months for Andrew: without the identity handed down by his family, he could not find an identity of his own. Yet the forced pause, during which Andrew had to put himself back together helped him have a clearer idea of where HE wanted to go to university the following year. It turned out that a less prestigious university was fine for him, in fact better suited to him than the one chosen by the family. This new, daring, choice, gave Andrew the freedom to be in touch with so far unexplored aspects of himself, different from his parents. This is a good example of a successful and relatively short piece of work which helped the young person do the separation/individuation work that had not been sufficiently done before.

It is clear that Andrew needed to do this work: his particular sensitivity and receptivity helped him find a way of managing and curbing his parents' expectations of him, in turn this gave him the distance from them, the 'breathing space' he so desperately needed.

Developing his own identity also helped Andrew to open a new channel of communication with his parents who gradually became more able to give their son more space/freedom to explore his own wishes and to make his own choices, with a bit less pressure on him to follow the family's path..

In some cases, it is not so much the identity of the parents and their families that is handed down to the young person but more specifically the identity of one of the parents. Usually, this reflects a dynamic which is at the core of the parental couple where there is a dominant, strong partner and a more passive one.

Another recurrent difficulty is when the identity of the young person is strongly influenced, at times almost defined, by a sibling. What seems to happen is that, in some family dynamics, one child takes on a prominent role; this could be due to the fact that the 'prominent child' is problematic and takes up a lot of the parent's emotional space, with the effect that other children have to become quite invisible.

This was the case of another patient of mine, Anna, a 21-year-old young woman whom I saw for a year. She came to me because, in spite of her intelligence and physical beauty, since an early age, she felt invisible – first of all to her parents but in general to the world. This feeling was bearable when she was a child, but it had become increasingly hard during adolescence and early adulthood. She could not find herself, as she once poignantly said to me: 'I am always my parent's daughter and my brother's sister but I don't know who I am!'.

Anna's older brother struggled with mental health problems throughout his childhood and adolescence. He was behind academically, he had great difficulties in making friends and in general in moving on in his life. In spite of the fact that Anna was younger, she was ahead of him, both academically, socially and emotionally. There was a big gap between the siblings – this was hard for her brother but also for her parents. In the family dynamic, her competence, her achievements were a painful reminder of her brother's struggles. Anna grew up with the idea that she had to be small, almost invisible: her needs, her ambitions, her skills, had to shrink in order to protect her brother and her parents. It was striking how everyone in the family, close and extended, kept referring to her as 'baby Anna', even when she was growing into a big teenager. She was not fully allowed to grow in stature and 'status'. Her sense of being invisible thus became a key aspect of her developing identity and a constant stumbling block in her self-confidence, in spite of her many accomplishments and her attractiveness, she still felt unseen. The work with

Anna was to help her challenge the family system and to enable her to own the visibility she deserved.

There could be instances in which the dominant child is not difficult but the opposite, extremely good, well-behaved, the one who can hold the parent's gaze. In this case, one of the siblings, usually the one closest in age to the 'perfect child', can feel under pressure to develop a 'reactive identity', either the opposite or the same, to the other sibling, the 'perfect one'. Both cases disrupt the development of a more genuine self.

If a sibling can generate this disruption so can a divorce of the parents when it becomes the focus of family life, to such an extent, at times, that the identity of the children tends to revolve around it. An acrimonious and long divorce can be toxic for the family and detrimental to the development of an identity which is separate and free from parental conflicts. I was struck by the complaint of an 18-year-old boy who in a recent session was able to voice his anger against 'all the divorce politics' between his two waring parents that dominated his life for many years and kept him as 'the child between the parents'. An adult patient of mine, Paul, whose childhood was dominated by his parents constant fighting, which led to their divorce, vividly remembers the impact that this domestic war had on himself and his older sister, how it affected their developing identities. He detached himself emotionally and became the passive appeaser of the situation. His sister on the other hand, was deeply triggered by the fighting parents, her role was to actively fight them/oppose them. It is interesting to note how vividly Paul can recognise these traits in himself and in his sister.

A new identity: the 'Temporary Outsider'

The psychotherapist and family therapist Anna Dartington who worked for many years in the Adolescent Department at the Tavistock Clinic, describes the condition of the adolescent in between childhood and adulthood, old and new, as 'a temporary outsider'.(Dartington, 1994). This position requires both a secure attachment to the family as well as a capacity to explore the world outside the family. It is a 'boundary position', between inside and outside the familiar world of 'home'. Dartington warns that if this on the border position is not achieved there can be a 'right in or right-out mentality': the 'right out' is a wrench from the family, whereas 'right in' is being stuck inside. In the former scenario, we might find young people who are in a state of constant rebellion against their parents, through acting out in various kinds: it could be, for example, conduct disorder, antisocial or delinquent behaviour, taking drugs, being over promiscuous, or taking risks. As clinicians, these are all common presentations with adolescents.

The latter scenario – the 'right-in' mentality – is problematic in a different way: these are the kids who find it hard to leave home – in the more worrying cases – they become very isolated, almost reclusive; some might develop phobias that limit their movement outside the home. This is also the case of those young people who tend to bypass the challenges of adolescence by spending a lot of time online, 'onlife', as Alessandra Lemma points out in her chapter.

When my 14-year-old patient, Charles, started therapy with me he was very much a 'right in' young adolescent. The middle of 3 children, his older brother was already in the midst of adolescence, while his younger sister was still protected by her childhood. The parents, in the middle of a bad divorce, brought Charles to me as they were concerned that he had become very quiet, and was always at home, with few friends. They noticed that out of the 3 children, he was 'the appeaser', the one who would continually strive to make his parents happy. This at times was a balancing act: Charles had to accommodate the needs of a domineering father and an emotionally fragile mother. His parents were convinced that Charles was bearing the brunt of their divorce and that he needed to be able to talk about it, hence the referral to me.

Charles's referral was still that of a child: he was brought to his first session by his father. It was clear that the 'remit' of the therapy, at least at the beginning, was set by the adults. They wanted Charles to explore the impact of their divorce – probably feeling both relieved and guilty by their decision. It wasn't clear at all whether he wanted to do this; I felt that he was again being 'the appeaser', doing what his parents asked him to his 14-year-old self was still absent.

In the first session, I explained to Charles that his parents thought that their divorce was causing him stress and were keen for him to talk about this: but I wished to know whether he was keen too. He hesitated then added that he wasn't sure it was the divorce. His parents used to fight all the time when they were together, but it was easier now that they lived apart. I wondered whether he wanted to speak to me. With some encouragement he was able to tell me that he felt something was bothering him; it wasn't specifically the divorce, he wasn't quite sure what it was. His feelings were making him feel guilty; it became clear that one aspect of this guilt had to do with his wish to distance himself from his parents and his fear that this would anger his father and overwhelm his mother. The underlying fear – one which I encounter regularly in my work with adolescents – was that all this turmoil might not be 'normal'.

The more Charles was able to explore these strange and new feelings and to accept them as 'normal', the more he could distance himself from the original remit set by his parents. The sessions quickly became his own and this is how the teenager gradually emerged. No longer in the family dynamics, the 'appeaser' of them, reluctant to let go of his young self but much more on the border position, he was still attached to the family but also interested in the world outside. Gradually, over the 2 years of work, Charles became more interested in his friends and he could take a few risks with girls; he sometimes challenged his father's authority and was less preoccupied about his mother's fragility. He could, for example, tell his father that he did not want to go to their country house every weekend, he wanted to spend time with his friends in the city where he lived. Although the fighting between his parents, mostly about the financial aspects of their divorce, did not improve, the relationship Charles had with them individually did. Charles was able to gradually come out of the 'family shell' without needing to break it: he could go in and out of it and this enabled him to grow into a healthy and perfectly 'normal' teenager…

As we have seen in these pages, the psychological work required to become a subject (Briggs, 2008) is considerable. It involves a difficult balance between loss and newness.

The challenge is to find a model which is an evolution, not a replica, of the one passed down by the parents, letting go of it without totally rejecting it – which is what we have seen Charles did with his parents. This is indeed a challenge for all parties involved: nothing is the same: the bedrock of childhood is now behind. The centrality of the parents, that guaranteed safety and certainties, is no longer absolute. New influences come to the fore, friends gain that central place, romantic relationships appear on the scene and impose their importance. New role models take the place of the old ones – all this generates instability and feelings of loss but at the same time also great excitement for what is ahead, for a new sense of 'who I am'.

Conclusion

I would like to end this chapter with a dream that Anna, the patient I mentioned before, brought to me towards the end of her therapy. The dream so vividly captures the coexistence in the young person of what comes from the parents and is partly lost and the new, recently formed identity that subsequently emerges. In previous sessions, Anna had mentioned two plants in her living room which had great significance to her: one was a Ficus that had been in her parents' living room for 30 years, and which they had bought before she was born. It had always been kept in the same position, in the same pot; it grew for a few years and then it remained at the same height kept the same height. To Anna, it represented 'the legacy of my parents, the continuity of their values'. The other plant was a Pothos, which she bought the year she returned home after university. In the dream, Anna is in the living room of her parents' house. Her Pothos is flourishing, its leaves are green and lush, full of 'exponential potential' – two words that so aptly describe her great potential. She notices that its branches are intertwined with those of the Ficus which by contrast, is growing quite old and withered. She feels saddened by the ageing Ficus but also rejuvenated by the growth of her plant. I don't think there is a better image to describe how an emerging identity, a young and vigorous growth, is a combination of old and new leaves, a flourishing plant, 'Ficus-Photus', ready to engage with life.

Bibliography

Anderson, R. and Dartington, A. (1988). *Facing it Out: Clinical Perspectives on Adolescent Disturbance*. London, Duckworths/Tavistock Series.

Arnett, J. (2004). *Emerging Adulthood: The Winding Road from the Late Teens through the Twenties.* Oxford, Oxford University Press.

Blos, P. (1962). *On Adolescence. A Psychoanalytic Interpretation*. New York, NY, Free Press.

Blos, P. (1967). 'The Second Individuation Process in Adolescence'. *Psychoanalytic Study of the Child*, 23: 162–186.

Blos, P. (1979). *The Adolescent Passage: Developmental Issues*. New York, NY, International Universities Press.

Brenman Pick, I. (1988). 'Adolescence: Its Impact on Patient and Analyst'. In: *Authenticity in the Psychoanalytic Encounter: The Work of Irma Brenman Pick*. London, Routledge.

Briggs, S. (2008). *Working with Adolescents and Young Adults: A Contemporary Psychodynamic Approach*. London, New York, Palgrave Macmillan.

Cahn, R. (1998). 'The Process of Becoming a Subject in Adolescence'. In: Perret-Catipovic, M. and Ladame, F. Eds. *Adolescence and Psychoanalysis: The Story and the History*. London, Karnac.

Cole, E.R. (2009). 'Intersectionality and Research in Psychology'. *American Psychologist*, 64: 170–180.

Dartington, A. (1994). 'Some Thoughts on the Significance of the Outsider in Families and Other Social Groups'. In: Box, S. Ed. *Crisis in Adolescence: Object Relations Therapy with the Family*. New York, Jason Aronson.

Erikson, E.H. (1968). *Identity, Youth and Crisis*. New York, NY, W.W. Norton.

Ferrer-Wreder, L. and Kroger, J. (2020). *Identity in Adolescence: The Balance Between Self and Other*. London, Routledge.

Hoxter, S. (1964). 'The Experience of Puberty'. *Journal of Child Psychotherapy*, 1: 13–26.

Kennedy, R. (2000). 'Becoming a Subject: Some Theoretical and Clinical Issues'. *International Journal of Psychoanalysis*, 81: 875–892.

Lemma, A. (2010). *Under the Skin: A Psychoanalytic Study of Body Modifications*. London, Routledge.

Lemma, A. (2015). *Minding the Body: The Body in Psychoanalysis and Beyond*. London, Routledge.

Lewin, V, Sharp, B. Eds. (2009). *Siblings in Development*. London, Karnac.

Meltzer, D. (1973). 'Identification and Socialization in Adolescence'. In: *Sexual States of Mind*. London, Karnack.

Meltzer, D. and Harris, M. (2011). *Adolescence: Talks and Papers by Donald Meltzer and Martha Harris*, ed. Williams, M. London, Karnac.

Miller, D. (1998). *The Age Between: Adolescents in a Disturbed Society*. London, Cornmarket/Hutchinson.

Rossouw, T., Wiwe, M. and Vrouva, J. (2021). *Mentalization-Based Treatment for Adolescents: A Practical Treatment Guide*. London, Routledge.

Sprince, J. (2009). 'The Devil and the Deep Blue Sea: Dyadic Narcissism and the Problem of Individuality'. *Journal of Child Psychotherapy*, 35(1): 13–31.

Waddell, M. (2018). *On Adolescence: Inside Stories*. London, Routledge.

Waddell, M. (1998). *Inside Lives: Psychoanalysis and the Growth of the Personality*. London, Duckworths/Tavistock Series.

Chapter 2

The devil and the deep blue sea

Gender stereotypes and the problem of individuation

Jenny Sprince

Introduction

> *What are little boys made of?*
> *Slugs and snails and puppy dogs' tails, and that are little boys made of.*
> *What are little girls made of?*
> *Sugar and spice and all things nice, and that are little girls made of.*
> (English nursery rhyme)

This traditional children's rhyme succinctly describes some of the unconscious phantasies about gender that derive from our earliest infantile experiences.

As babies, we begin our lives as part of our mother's body; although we achieve physical separation at birth, it takes us longer to achieve psychological separation.

Becoming a separate individual is a complicated process. Forming a sense of gender identity is an important part of that process, and the differentiation between little girls and little boys that is described in the rhyme represents an early stage of this achievement. Gender stereotyping is typical of a very early developmental stage, where the mother gives blissful attunement and the father unwanted separateness and individuation. As the baby develops into a child, the dyad with the mother is less necessary, and the child becomes interested in what is outside and different from the mother; this is the beginning of the individuation process which includes otherness. It generally starts with the father.

Early development

In the earliest phase of development, mother and baby are entirely focused on each other, mirroring one another in a state of psychological twinship. When mother's attentiveness is withdrawn, or when the baby experiences anxieties for which mother cannot or does not provide emotional containment[1], the baby regresses in phantasy to a still earlier stage of development. This is a stage of fusion, where the baby is still a part of the mother, and there is no differentiation.

For the first months of their lives, babies live in a world dominated by their mother and her attributes. This affects their early preconception of gender and

DOI: 10.4324/9781003351184-3

gender-specific body parts. Mother's breast is an all-providing cornucopia – 'sugar and spice, and all things nice'. In the 'twinship' between the mother and her infant, father's presence is often felt as an unnecessary appendix, irrelevant to the mother/baby dyad. His participation can be ignored, despised, or ridiculed: a 'slug or a snail or a puppy dog's tail'. This has important consequences for little boys; later, they may take a defensive position, over-valuing a part of themselves that was previously denigrated, or be predisposed to feelings of shame and disgust about their masculinity.

In benign circumstances, this phase of development, where mother and baby are twinned, is relatively brief. It is followed by the recognition of being separate, and the exploration of the mother and her other relationships. As father and siblings come increasingly into focus, the baby realizes that these other relationships do exist and sometimes take the mother's attention elsewhere. Father and his masculine potency, symbolically represented by his penis, can be felt as an intrusive and dangerous interference. In psychoanalytic thinking the idealised penis of the father is called the phallus: its attributes are potency and autonomy.

If this recognition causes anxieties that the baby's mother does not or cannot alleviate, the baby will regress to the earlier stage of narcissistic twinning, a stage that excludes other relationships and impedes individuation. In benign circumstances, however, as the baby approaches toddlerhood he or she will make use of a growing identification with father and other external family members to promote differentiation from mother.

It is during this developmental stage that gender stereotyping and polarisation emerge: mother and her breast come to represent states of attunement, twinship and fusion, while father comes to represent separateness and individuation. For the toddler, trying literally to stand on his own two feet, these latter qualities become increasingly valuable.

Where, in an earlier phase, mother's breast was idealised as the source of all comfort and safety, now it is the turn of the father and his phallus; its idealised potency symbolises the ability to manage without mother and her breast, to be independent of everything that the breast represents, and to have a mind of one's own.

This is the stage when, in benign circumstances, little girls may become envious of their brothers' penises, rather than smug about their own lack of one.

In normal development both boys and girls may feel that they can possess this idealised penis, just as both boy and girl babies feel twinned with the idealised breast. In most nurseries you can see little girls dressing up as fairy queens with magical phallic wands; while little boys play with phallic guns and try on their big sisters' dresses. This stage of identification with one or both primitive gender stereotypes is a necessary preparation for understanding oneself and others in a world peopled by both men and women.

In reality, none of us can possess either idealised attribute, let alone both. However, boys can more easily believe themselves able to own the phallus because of their ownership of a penis, just as girls can believe that they will one day own an idealised, all-providing breast.

For both boys and girls, the move to the phallus represents an achievement. It marks a stage where individuation from mother, being outside and different from her, feels more exciting than dangerous, and where the mutual exploration of difference can begin to form the foundation for making loving relationships. This is why, every bit as much as boys, girls may struggle if they have been given inadequate support in their phallic identification and functioning.

For example, a young girl, Tessa, found it hard to develop an appropriately separate relationship with her mother and could not be induced to go to school. She brought the following image regularly to her psychotherapy sessions: she was adrift on a turbulent sea and was clinging for life to a single insubstantial branch. I came to understand this branch as Tessa's ways of representing her identification with a weak but well-meaning father, who found it hard to rescue her from an over-dependent relationship with her powerful and needy mother.

In order to overcome the pull back to the early twinship with the mother, and from there to a phantasy of fusion, certain conditions need to be met: children need to know that they can return to a safe place inside mother's mind, that they can continue to push their passionate feelings into her, and that she will not respond with rejection, anger or dismay. But they also need to know that she – or some other trusted adult – will provide the masculine/phallic functioning that will allow them to recover their separate individuality. This means that they will not be trapped in a terrifying state of fusion, where all possibility of differentiation has been submerged. Good mothers provide this reassurance instinctively.

For instance, an angry four-year-old became visibly jealous because his mother was attending to his baby sister rather than to him. He picked up a cushion and threw it at his mother's face. His mother put the cushion back on the sofa and said, 'Come on, Harry, calm down. I know I haven't given you enough attention today: don't worry, I promise I'll make time for you later.' Harry calmed down.

Harry had differentiated himself from his mother sufficiently to be angry with her; this was possible because he trusted that she would understand his jealousy towards his sister and that she would come to his rescue, with a gentle but firm response which contained his feelings. This enabled Harry to choose a soft cushion to throw at her, rather than the toy building block that was nearer to hand.

The gender stereotypes that underpin these symbolic attributes – maternal and paternal – are not necessarily dependent on the concrete presence of a male/female couple. Tessa's father and mother were unable – either individually or as a couple – to provide her with a symbolic marriage between masculine and feminine functioning. On the other hand, Harry's mother was a single parent.[2]

A child of either gender who has had sufficient experience of the symbolic marriage of these functions will attain intuitive respect for both masculine and feminine attributes, and will be better able to cope with ordinary Oedipal jealousies, as well as differences of gender, opinion and personality.

In less benign circumstances, these developments may not be easy for a baby to achieve. If mother's anxieties are such that she rejects the baby's attempts at differentiation; if she cannot respond with compassion and understanding to negative emotions; if mother sees father and the outside world as persecuting rather than exciting; if the world beyond mother presents real threats to mother and baby – in any of these circumstances the dangers of emerging from a fused or twinned state may feel too great. This is likely to have repercussions in later life.

Adolescence

The anxieties of puberty exacerbate primitive gender polarisation, and, simultaneously, the pull backwards towards twinship and fusion with others. Adolescent boys and girls show a tendency to regress into polarised gender stereotypes, much as nursery age children do. Boys will group together in displays of phallic narcissism, while girls will display an equivalent narcissism, based on their identification with an idealised, alluring breast.

Among adults too, in everyday life, we see examples of such gender stereotyping all around us. There is a valency in men and women to favour their own gender identifications: thus, women will tend to prioritise attunement, conformity and dependency, whilst men will tend to prioritise individuation, differentiation and the capacity to surmount emotional and physical neediness. In certain circumstances, and in single gender groups, this tendency can create extremes of gender narcissism. In women this may lead to a denial of all negative feelings; in men this may lead to an attack on all dependency needs.

As adults, we hope to form partnerships that help to correct these tendencies and steer us towards a middle position.

Typically, however, when two young people first fall in love, they recapitulate the experience of the mother–baby dyad, mirroring one another in a state of attuned twinship: 'two minds with but a single thought, two hearts that beat as one.' They may struggle to allow one another room to be separate individuals in a way that parallels the struggles of infancy.

But, all being well, the experience of forming a couple will consolidate a development beyond gender stereotyping: partners will learn to see one another as individuals with identifications that span both genders. An understanding of the good collaboration between the masculine and the feminine part will moderate the reliance on identification with a stereotypically idealised masculinity and femininity.This in turn, will enhance the couple's potential for good triadic functioning, facilitating the development of adult collaboration within parenthood, and the acceptance of the differences within the couple.

But the pull towards twinship and fusion continues throughout our lives, and is felt more powerfully within large groups and organisations; where these organisations provide care for troubled adolescents, they offer particularly valuable insights into the primitive gender stereotypes that are associated with these earliest phases of development (Birksted-Breen, 1996).

The clinical observations that follow are derived from my work as a child psychotherapist and psychodynamic organisational consultant within a variety of settings. For the sake of simplicity and to protect identities, I have compressed them into two fictional organisations: 'Crawford House' and 'Selbury Manor.'

Gender stereotypes in a single gender community: Crawford house

Crawford House was a residential boarding school for adolescent boys with emotional and behavioural difficulties, staffed predominantly by male teachers and care workers.

The psychotherapy room was isolated, at the far end of the building, and the staff sent me a series of large, violent adolescent boys, who arrived with knives and cigarette lighters, trashed the furniture, and tried to strangle me.

In the staffroom, I found myself at the centre of challenging banter: what was the good of 'all this touchy-feely stuff'? they asked me. What these boys really needed was good, firm discipline. Lots of football with a tough referee, who punished fouls and got them to join together as a team. They needed cold showers. They didn't respond well to softness: a female member of the care staff team, who had tried that, had had her car windows smashed in. I felt that these comments were intended to shock and intimidate me.

Other women were treated with similar contempt. One female teacher was off sick for a week, and was asked, on her return, whether she ought not to consider leaving as she 'obviously hadn't got what it takes'. Meanwhile, a male teacher who suffered from regular migraines was only gently teased for his frequent absences: he was affectionately accused of skiving, or of having been out boozing and suffering from a week-long hangover. All of this mirrored similar behaviours towards or amongst the boys. I heard of frequent outbreaks of sexualised bullying: gangs of boys would pick on a weaker, less assertively 'masculine' boy and beat him up, or pull down his trousers. That worse didn't happen amongst the children was due to an almost military system of constant supervision.

I could see how the school's picture of femininity related to the experiences of the children. Most boys had come from a background of domestic violence or sexual abuse; their hatred and contempt for mothers who had colluded with the behaviour of abusive fathers or prioritised them over their sons was palpable. I felt constantly assaulted by images of women as brittle or flaccid, easily raped and pillaged, with no strength or elasticity to resist or respond. There seemed to be little concept of a potent female sexuality and no concept at all of a male sexuality that wasn't equated with peeing, defecating and destructive intrusion.

I came to think of this culture of phallic narcissism as a defensive manoeuvre designed to counter a picture of masculinity that entailed so much shame and guilt; and this understanding helped me to find a compassionate response. I learned fast to find appropriate forms of banter designed to reassure both the boys and the men that I didn't find their masculinity disgusting, dangerous, or threatening. This won me respect within individual relationships, but it had little impact on the culture as a whole.

Gender stereotypes in a mixed gender community: Selbury manor

I had an idea of how masculinity and femininity were perceived by such organisations before I started work in a therapeutic community, which I will call Selbury Manor. Yet I was unprepared for the extent to which these stereotypes were rigidly enforced by a staff group composed of equal numbers of sophisticated young men and women, and a mixed group of boys and girls.

The director at Selbury Manor, Jonathan, was a thoughtful and compassionate man, very keen to promote a culture that would empower both genders. So it was bewildering to observe how, both in staff meetings and in the daily community meetings, he was regularly provoked into a furious row with one or other of the senior men, or into shouting matches with one of the boys, whilst the women and the girls remained silent.

In one community meeting, for example, Jonathan challenged two of the older boys over some unacceptable behaviour. They tried to justify themselves and he refused to listen to their justification. When they swore at him, he shouted back, telling them not to dare use that kind of language with him. Afterwards they came up to me to ask me what I thought: did I blame them for saying 'fuck'? I said, cautiously, that I thought perhaps they wanted me to understand that they'd felt hurt by Jonathan's refusal to listen to their explanation. One of them responded, with great vehemence: 'Yes! Like when the hammer hits your thumb when you're trying to hammer in a nail, you don't just say "Oh dearie me!"'

Amongst these phallic hammers, competing for dominance, the females seemed insignificant and powerless. The men on the staff seemed to collude with the boys in a contemptuous belief that the women were weak, useless and stupid. Here is one example.

Karen, a junior member of staff, had been set upon by a gang of children who punched and bruised her. In a staff discussion meeting, she said how upset she felt about how people had treated her the next day. Everyone seemed to despise her: senior members of staff had implied it was her own fault. She was prepared to think it might be, but in what way? Nobody seemed to want to give her an answer.

Eventually, male staff members began to question her about her own past, hinting that they suspected that she had been sexually abused as a girl. As she became upset, I intervened, saying that I thought she was getting beaten up all over again. The staff were silent for a time. Then someone said that her fragility reminded him of his mother and made him angry. This led to a discussion about what 'fragility' meant. No one seemed able to offer anything but a physical definition.

Karen said she had been trying to reprimand a child when the gang had set on her. Wasn't that the opposite of being fragile? No, said another of the men: she shouldn't have got into a confrontation in the first place – it was just provocative. Karen pointed out that she was now being told not just that she was 'fragile' but that she ought to stay that way. 'No', said the man, angrily, 'but it's silly to get into a confrontation when you know you can't win.'

'You think I ought to be fragile just because I'm not a man,' said Karen. There were nods from several of the other women.

Dangerous femininity

I thought it was striking that the culture of phallic narcissism that was obstinately maintained – a belief in fragile females and powerful males – was at odds with facts that I discovered through individual conversations – facts that were never publicly discussed or acknowledged. For instance, one of the girls had recently caused a serious car crash by a sexual attempt on the driver; another had committed a near fatal stabbing; and several of them had taken an active part in the violent attack on Karen.

When I began to point this out, and to wonder aloud about frightening, powerful and aggressive mothers, I encountered a stunned silence. Then, slowly, the adults began to explore what was known about the children's mothers, and the accounts of psychiatric illness, violence, abuse and neglect that were recorded in the files. At first, the staff seemed to react to this new thought with interest, but little emotional engagement. Then, within a few weeks, a female teaching assistant came to work in a florid delusional state and had to be sectioned. Other adults revealed that she had secretly been on long-term anti-psychotic medication, and suggested that she had wilfully stopped taking it, as a consequence of our discussions. When I wondered with Jonathan about the meaning of this, he responded by telling me in confidence about a previous female member of staff who had had what he described as a break-down: one night, when they were both sleeping in, she had come into his bedroom with her pyjama top unbuttoned, exposing her breasts to him.

I found myself feeling that I was being 'warned off': if I dared to challenge the accepted view of fragile but benign femininity, I would be inviting an outbreak of rampant female sexuality and psychosis. These experiences made me re-evaluate my thinking about Crawford. Was the unconscious hypothesis that men and boys needed a powerful phallus in order to cope with the threat of female madness, mal-evolence and seductiveness? It seemed that at Selbury Manor, too, women had to be kept in their place, subjugated to the firm dominance of the men.

But this did not appear to apply to me in my role as a consultant. On the contrary, the staff seemed suspiciously ready to idealise me. This took the form of an apparent paralysis: it seemed that I was expected to do all their thinking for them. The force of this expectation often paralysed me, as well.

Here is an example. During our regular staff discussion forum, the care worker who had been left to monitor the children put his head round the door: the children were trying to walk on the frozen lake, and the ice wasn't very solid, he said. What ought he to do? No one responded and eventually he went away. He came back a few minutes later, looking desperate. This time, I found the strength to comment about the madness of leaving the children to fall through the ice, with only one adult to attend to them. My intervention seemed to be greeted with some surprise, but it did result in members of the group going to the rescue.

I felt that a group phantasy was being demonstrated: the staff seemed to assume that our discussion meeting was so important that it outweighed the necessity of keeping the children safe. Who had I become in their minds, I wondered, when they believed that I would think so, too?

I understood this incident as a re-enactment of the earliest infant-mother dyad, where the mother and baby – in this case, myself and the group – are merged in mutual narcissism at the expense of others and to their own inevitable detriment.

All anxiety was to be kept outside the door, for someone else to cope with, whilst the group and I enjoyed our euphoric communion.

I call this state 'dyadic narcissism'. It is the prolongation of this state that gives rise to the extremes of phallic narcissism that I had witnessed both at Crawford House and at Selbury Manor. The unconscious logic is: children get out of hand because women are mad and dangerous. They seduce others into a state of mindless euphoria. The solution is that men should eschew dependency needs; teach boys to control women; require women to be endlessly accommodating; and ensure that they are never trusted with potency of any kind. In return, and so long as women keep in line, men will agree to accord them protection and a limited measure of respect.

Dyadic narcissism

I soon noticed that this phenomenon of dyadic narcissism was one that was regularly repeated throughout the institution. Within the staff discussion groups, we started to examine it more closely.

Although occurring often amongst both genders, it usually showed itself when at least one member of the dyad was a female. We rarely observed it between two males. If the boys got together, it was more often to attack other children, or the staff, or the fabric of the building.

Here is a vignette to illustrate this relationship between two adolescent girls.

Sandra and Ayesha – both fifteen – are inseparable. They make a point of dressing in similar clothes. They go everywhere together, arm-in-arm. Their friendship is claustrophobic in its intensity. The boys in their peer group find it sexually provocative; they get 'high as kites' – quite literally: they climb out on the roof and attempt to clamber in at Ayesha's or Sandra's bedroom windows. When the staff intervene, they attack them. But whenever such things happen, Ayesha and Sandra deny any part in it: they never asked the boys to behave like that!

Eventually, a boy describes how he has heard Ayesha instructing Sandra on how to punish a younger boy who tried to make friends with her: 'Tell him to walk on the ice,' she'd said, 'and then walk away and let him drown.' 'She did it, too!' says one of the girls. 'I saw her. She took him down to the lake and dared him to walk on the ice where it's frozen – it's too thin for that, he'd have fallen in!'

Dyadic relationships like these work to very strict rules – an unspoken contract – that neither side is allowed to contravene. The rules seem to be as follows:

- Each party will rely on the other for all emotional satisfaction.
- There must be no other really significant attachment beyond the dyad.
- No difference of opinion or taste can be tolerated.
- Thinking for oneself is treachery.
- Anyone who tries to intervene or disrupt the dyad is cruel, insensitive or just plain stupid. They deserve no compassion.
- All unacceptable feelings that might otherwise belong within the relationship – hatred, contempt, rivalry, envy – will be disowned and projected into those beyond the dyad.
- The discomfort of being trapped within this claustrophobic dyad will also be disowned and projected. However, it is permissible to manipulate others to disrupt the dyad, and then punish them for it.

We can infer from these rules how dangerous the consequences of differentiation can feel to a baby in the earliest months of life.

Conclusion

The baby's state of total dependency makes it hard for him or her to develop beyond the earliest stages of fusion and twinned identification with the mother. Anyone beyond the dyad who threatens to interrupt this blissful communion may be experienced as abusive. If this phase is unduly prolonged, it will inhibit the baby's development of a separate identity. The baby needs to be offered encouragement, reassurance and permission for phallic identifications. If this is not provided, the relationship with the mother will be experienced as claustrophobic and become increasingly untenable.

In these circumstances, children can feel caught between the devil and the deep blue sea: between identification with an abusive phallus and a seductive breast. They must choose between taking sadistic control, in order to liberate themselves, or risking the annihilation of the self.

This dilemma can lead boys and men into a state of mind in which they feel compelled to control and silence women, and to repudiate dependency and empathy. It can lead girls and women into a parallel state of mind where they can insist on their right to own both the breast and the phallus, while denying and projecting their own phallic functioning. They can become covertly tyrannical and manipulative in ways that may be hard to recognise and challenge, while still insisting on their undivided loyalty to an idealised breast.

But although these are extreme examples, we all carry some vestiges of these primitive identifications.

Every baby struggles to achieve individuation, and has at some point projected into the breast the desire to stay merged. We have all experienced the breast, in phantasy, as seductive and castrating, luring us back into a state of twinship, and from there into a state of fusion; we have all needed to achieve some measure of phallic functioning in order to differentiate, to achieve a sense of self and permission to think our own thoughts and feel our own feelings.

In benign circumstances, this process is supported by a mother who can bear the loss of early idealisation; and by a father who can lovingly tolerate the symbiotic dyad from which he is temporarily excluded, and can encourage the gradual process of differentiation through a loving engagement with both mother and baby[3].

Where differentiation has been adequately supported, the baby's symbiotic identification with mother alternates with an identification with a father who represents the possibility of differentiation, and can tolerate the toddler's hostility; and where mother has been supported in a loving relationship with father, the toddler can identify with both sets of attributes. These attributes can then be conjoined into a separate entity: the benign differentiated parental couple from which he or she is sometimes excluded.

This triangulation creates the potential for autonomous thinking and the development of curiosity and respect. And along the way, it allows us to grow beyond our earliest and most primitive understanding of the meaning of gender.

Notes

1 'Containment' is a technical term within psychoanalytic thinking: it describes a process of empathic understanding coupled with a thoughtful and compassionate response.
2 I do not have space here to explore the issue of sexual orientation, and the many reasons why a child's sense of gender identity and eventual choice of gender in a sexual partner may not conform to the heterosexual norm. In my experience, gender stereotyping has equal importance within both heterosexual and homosexual development: it derives from phantasy rather than concrete reality. A successful marriage of masculine and feminine functioning is possible within both orientations.
3 A parallel process applies to same-sex partnerships.

Bibliography

1. Birksted-Breen, D. 1996. 'Phallus, penis and mental space'. *International Journal of Psycho-Analysis*, 77: 649–657.
2. Freud, S. 1923. 'The infantile genital organisation'. *SE*, 19: 139–145.
3. Freud, S. 1924. 'The dissolution of the Oedipus complex'. *SE*, 19: 172–179.
4. Freud, S. 1925. 'Some psychological consequences of the anatomical distinction between the sexes'. *SE*, 19: 241–258.

Chapter 3

Preadolescence

The silence of words and the words of the body

Franco D'Alberton

Introduction

There is a period in a parent's life in which interactions with the son or daughter suddenly become problematic. And this is not when, almost as a physiological component of the relationship, adolescents express their need to establish distance through confrontations and demands of autonomy from parents who are "different" than those with whom they had when they were children. Instead, I am referring to the period that is structured around the stimulus of puberty, when the child demonstrates maturity involving the body, the mind, the hormonal system, and thus sexuality.

David Grossman (2002) describes with the power of his poetic text what happens in this period from the point of view of the kids.

"I think of the solitude of the individual who, suddenly at the age of twelve or thirteen, receives a physiological signal and enters a kind of tunnel, from which he will emerge after five or six years. And while the adolescent finds himself in this tunnel, his soul and his body are completely subject to the tyranny of biological processes, to the arbitrary action of the glands, and at bottom, he is completely alone, as though in a nightmare in which he helplessly observes the incredible changes happening to him, totally independent of his control.[1]

A sudden growth, in which the body and the mind follow varying developmental timelines, begins to give shape to a subsequent central theme of adolescence to come: integration of the sexual body into the adolescent's representation of himself (Laufer and Laufer 1984).

Physical contact with sons and daughters, which had been an important modality of communication, with hugs, warm-heartedness, and play involving contact, begins to pose problems for parents as well, who struggle to keep the same level of physicality with children who have suddenly become men and women, even though, still unaware of the change, they continue to behave as they did earlier.

Boys and girls begin to experience their first autonomous pursuits at this age, with a consequent near-devotion to cell phones: "You'll have a cell phone when you go to school alone." It often happens that one sees these boys and girls, now in secondary school, going to school while clutching a cell phone as though it were a

DOI: 10.4324/9781003351184-4

compass, almost as though they were looking for directions about which streets to take from home to school, a route they do every day. It is as if the phone validates their actions. It represents a sign of status of belonging, a need for security which makes them grip a concrete object that fulfills transitional functions they are, in search of certainties about the self and their placement in the world (Sugarman 2017). Sometimes in a group, the Smartphone serves as a way to share texts and music, dance steps, and new interests in a culture that differentiates itself from the familiar, allowing the channeling of curiosity and instinctual energies in a socially shared way. In other moments, Smartphones help young people to remain connected, tied together with chats and conversations that give the impression of being in a real group, posting and receiving even intimate images or visiting pornographic sites, in a way that is often underestimated by adults (D'Alberton & Scardovi, 2021).

Preadolescence is an age in which impulses antithetical to the self are present. On the one hand, this leads young people to detach from the parents and strive for autonomy, while on the other, a sense of inner emptiness connected to loss of security in the relationship with the parents – the security that was experienced during childhood, that is – pushes them toward a renewed urge for closeness and to the need for intimate contact. This happens especially with mothers and is expressed in ways that are typical of much younger children. "Don't hang over me" is a request for autonomy that is often closely followed by "in this house, no one loves me" . There is a new push toward autonomy, immediately followed by the need to go back to something known and to a closeness – physical as well – that tends to rekindle contact with the parents.

Furthermore, this is an especially difficult period for the parents as well, who – through their children's experiences – tend to relive moments that they themselves experienced in their relationship with the parents of their childhood and adolescence. Longstanding ties or ancient conflicts can be reactivated depending on how things went in the course of parent's developmental journey. A moment of particular difficulty, the encounter with their children's pubertal development, strongly tests the skill of being a parent.

The clinical vignettes and the reflections expressed in this paper come from psychological consultation work carried out in a pediatric hospital at the request of pediatricians who were confronting situations in which, despite significant symptomatology, there was a powerful emotional component (see D'Alberton 2017, 2018).

Notes on puberty

As alluded to earlier, puberty is the period of growth that signals the end of childhood, when boys and girls experience physiological and psychological changes of great significance. Sudden and rapid growth leads them to reach their adult height and the maturity of the sexual organs, with the arrival of fertility and secondary sexual characteristics.

The elements that determine its onset are controlled by the neuroendocrine system through a complex network of excitatory and inhibitory factors that are in large part still unknown, remaining one of the mysteries of human biology. They stem from a complex interaction between genetic and environmental factors, thanks to which, during the last century, we have seen the age of the onset of puberty shift approximately three years earlier (Parent, Franssen, Fudvoye 2015).

The sexual hormones, already present in embryonic phases and reaching the peak of their production during the first 15 to 20 days after birth, are maintained at very low levels throughout childhood, until the beginning of puberty, when they are reactivated with the awakening of activity of the hypothalamus-hypophysis-gonad axis (Kuiri-Hänninen, Sankilampi, Dunkel 2014).

The first physical sign of the advent of puberty in the male body, with the influx of hypophysial gonadotropins, is the increase in testicular volume, which can happen between the ages of 9 and 14, with the average age being 11½. In the female, it is estrogenic ovarian activity, again stimulated by the gonadotropins, which promote development of the mammary buds between the ages of 8 and 13, with an average age of 10½.

In both the boy and the girl, contrary to what one might think, the appearance of axillary and pubic hair does not necessarily coincide with the onset of puberty; in fact, this is the expression of another hormonal process connected to the production of androgens on the part of the adrenal gland and can happen before ovarian or testicular activation.

In addition to the one-year-earlier average age of pubertal onset in girls, the rhythm of development itself is different in the two sexes. This is what quickly emerges when we observe secondary school students. We can see sudden growth spurts over the course of only a few months, with a tendency that frequently leads girls to complete their physical development while boys are still at the beginning.

This is due to the fact that the rate of growth in height during puberty increases in speed and reaches its apex at differing times in females and males, owing to the action of estrogens – responsible for bone growth – available to girls from the beginning of puberty, while in boys, testosterone is transformed into estrogen during a later period. Thus, in addition to the later onset of puberty, the growth spurt in the boy occurs about a year later as well.

The entire process of growing taller in puberty is completed in four to five years, for an average total growth of 30 to 31 centimeters in boys and 27.5 to 29 centimeters in girls. During the period of accelerated growth in height, which contributes 17% to 18% of a person's final height, the increase in height in boys is about 9.5 centimeters per year, and in girls it is 8.5 centimeters per year (Abbassi 1998).

In summary, the boys puberty involves important growth and arrival at his adult height; a change in bodily composition, with an increase in thin muscle mass; and the development of the genitals, with an increase in the volume of the testicles and the length of the penis, in addition to the first ejaculation.

In girls, growth and reaching adult stature are accompanied by a modification in bodily composition and an increase in fat mass, as well as by the development of the breasts and the genital apparatus, with the appearance of the first menstruation (Abreu and Kaiser 2016).

In terms of brain functioning, it has been shown that development of cerebral configuration cannot be considered to have terminated before the end of adolescence and arrival at the age of adulthood. According to neuroscientists, the adolescent brain has reached 80% of its maturation (Jensen 2014), and the prefrontal lobes – responsible for an increase in abstract reasoning, attentional capacity, the inhibitory capacities, linguistic control, and the control and planning of behaviors – are the last to mature (Giedd 2015).

In practice, from a biological point of view, biological and sexual maturity precedes social and psychological maturity, which as we shall see, requires an enduring task of integrating bodily changes into the representation that the adolescent will have of himself. This allows us to look into the psychoanalytic point of view in which puberty is seen as triggering the second period of infantile sexuality, around which adolescent dynamics take shape.

The first period of sexuality unfolds in psychosexual phases, from birth up to more or less the age of beginning primary school, and leads children to encounter oedipal dynamics. From then onward, the earlier instinctual energy dedicated to curiosity about one's own body and the bodies of others becomes available for learning and knowledge, in what is defined as the latency phase (Freud 1905). This period is characterized by a certain quiescence in the push of the drives, which are temporarily subordinated to the demands of superego ideals, which in turn lead to the desire to know and to recognition of the difference between sexes and between generations. It is a period that accompanies the child to the threshold of puberty.

For Anna Freud, what characterizes the phase that follows, preadolescence, is a quantitative increase in the drives, with the representation of their pregenital characteristics and of fantasies that characterized the expression of sexuality in infancy. There is an instinctual pressure, violent and irregular, in which the thrust of the drive at times expresses an amount of sensorial stimuli that exceeds the ego's capacities, which risks overwhelming the developing mind's capacity to psychically work through the somatic and relational changes.

The "pubertal," as Gutton (1991) calls the journey that represents "the equivalent for the psyche of what puberty is for the body," can take on an intensity that is at times excessive, potentially traumatic. In other words, at this age, we can imagine the mind as a container with a funnel over it, whose neck, represented by the mental competence of working through, can process only a certain amount of the sensorial elements stemming from transformations in the body and in relationships. The excessive amount, unable to get inside the container of mental working through, can assume traumatic characteristics, threatening the balance and the previous emotional security or overflowing in the body.

Pubertal development gives new meaning to memories and experiences of earlier phases, the discovery of sexual emotions and excitement in one's own body also influences relationships with the parents. Additionally, the need for autonomy is reinforced by the urgent need to avoid the anxiety of an overly intense connection with persons whose physical nearness takes on sexual characteristics.

The world of childhood and its connections, in particular with the parents, is now marked by an anxiety-provoking sexuality and a sexual maturity which reactivates old oedipal phantasies. While earlier on, the parents – even at times of conflict – were considered stable sources of security, immutable Herculean columns in the known relational world, they are now suddenly of little interest, scarcely meaningful and having "the shabby proportions of a fallen idol" (Blos 1962, p. 91). This is something that is not easy for the preadolescent, and that leads him to experience a feeling of depressive grief in relation to the parents of his childhood, "he experiences the inner emptiness, grief, and sadness which is part of all mourning" (Blos 1962, p. 100). This painful process can be completed only gradually.

The fallout from these complicated changes, both physical and mental, emphasizes the gap between narcissistic investments which provide stability to the self-state, and object investments, which pertain to the relationship with the object and to drive satisfaction. The balance between object investments and narcissistic ones is part of a journey that began long ago, – in the early years of life, within the first caregiving connections, where, if all goes well, the infant begins to feel secure. This feeling is what then allows children to manage separation, being separate, to gradually become autonomous and capable of integrating their own instinctual urges in various phases of their development.

In other words, this is a *process of subjectification,* as Cahn (2006, 2009) defines the journey that unfolds throughout the course of life. This is the process that leads the little human being to become a subject, starting from the way in which his early needs come to be recognized and reinforced within primary relationships.

The early feeling of being alive and meaningful to others allows the child to cope with subsequent stages of growth, with the awareness of being separate. He gradually learns how to overcome the phantasy of fusion with the mother, how to accept the presence of a third. The aim to achieve, at the end of the libidinal phases of child development, a capacity to contain the innate desire for union with the parent of the opposite sex, to recognize the limits of childhood omnipotence, to accept the difference between the sexes and the gap between generations.

Along this journey, the preadolescent is exposed to a crucial conflict between the necessity of maintaining one's own sense of identity and security, consolidated within the relationship with the parents over the course of childhood, and opening himself to the desire for the other. This involves the fear of consigning to that other the "keys" to his own self, as well as the fear of a loss of borders, of being invaded and colonized by one's own objects of desire (see Jeammet [2007] on the narcissistic-objectual disparity).

Body and thought in formation

Blos (1962) divides the entire adolescent journey into five phases: preadolescence, early adolescence, actual adolescence, late adolescence, and post-adolescence.

This paper is dedicated especially to the first of these, preadolescence, which, with the stimulus of puberty, irrevocably introduces a profound break with childhood.

In this phase, generally from 10 to 14 years, it is mostly the body that lends itself to the expression of a discomfort of which youngsters and their families struggle to grasp the emotional origins; this discomfort stems from the charged impact of the powerful pubertal sensoriality on thinking structures that are still fragile (De Ajuraguerra 1974; Cramer 1977; Kreisler 1981; Lebovici 1985).

The functional somatic or somatoform disturbances consist of a heterogeneous group of conditions that, inexplicable from a medical point of view, can pose significant problems for the medical authorities to which families usually refer to before turning to psychological or psychotherapeutic resources (Luyten, Van Houdnhove, Lemma, Target, Fonagy 2012, 2013). Abdominal pains are one of their main expressions, with a symptomatology at times so pronounced that it is difficult to imagine the lack of an organic cause. At other times, there are cephalgias, fevers, dizzy spells, there are various forms of asthenia that impede boys and girls from controlling their legs; this can understandably provoke the fear, in parents and doctors, of serious forms of neurological pathologies. There are respiratory disturbances or episodes of paroxysmal and persistent coughing that have incapacitating effects by day, yet at night they mysteriously disappear (Campo 2001; D'Alberton 2004, 2017, 2018; Brunelli, Balzani, Briganti 2006; Carbone 2009, 2010; Schulte 2011; Casini 2015).

Bodily changes related to growth and sexual development involve a major upset in the psychological balance established in childhood; they require intense psychic work on the part of the preadolescent to adapt himself to these sudden modifications. Significantly, these occur at a time in which, at a mental level, very broad, unexplored horizons are opening up through the acquisition of formal operational capacities of hypothetical, deductive thinking; that is, it is now possible to carry out mental operations while setting aside concrete facts (Piaget 1964). If those reality-based facts were necessary up until the threshold of puberty, from then on, young people become ever more capable of actualizing formal operations – of reasoning on the basis of hypotheses, of imagining every possible theoretical scenario. These new mental processes provide intellectual autonomy that goes hand in hand with the need for autonomy, almost a 'liberation' from parental figures.

Parents and children: Intervention hypotheses

In reviewing requests for consultation received from pediatricians over the years, with the goal of evaluating possible emotional problems underlying symptomatology expressed via the body, one notices that, almost without exception, these requests have related to children either of secondary school age or during the first years of life. These are the two major periods in which the body lends itself to expressing psychological dynamics. Indeed, one could say that a substantial affinity exists between the way that an individual has coped with the first steps of life, and how he will face the journey that will lead him to become an autonomous and mature person. The parents' involvement in both these periods becomes essential because, in confronting preadolescent problems, it is often possible to identify fault lines in the emotional and relational development of the early years of life.

From the consultations requested for those conditions and similar ones, treatments have ranged from a single encounter with the parents and/or the children, to multiple meetings, up to the point of individual psychotherapy sessions or group meetings held with preadolescents, often accompanied by individual or group meetings with their parents as well.

The physiological transformation of what we have seen as representative of "pubertal violence", whose objective is the working through of incestuous phantasies through symbolization and mental representation – does not depend only on the adolescent's internal capacities. It also relies on "narcissistic parental support" (Gutton 2000) within **the** "broadened psycic space" (Jeammet 2007) defined by the adolescent's need for his parents to actively support the pubertal process and the subsequent adolescent phase. This support isn't always easy to provide, because the child's puberty can reactivate unresolved conflicts in the relationship with his parents, the symptomatology of which can express transgenerational suffering already evident in interactions during the early years of the child's life.

Their sons' and daughters' adolescent development constitutes an important journey of growth for parents as well, one in which the dynamics of the single individuals, those of the couple and of the entire family are tested to their limit. This is especially true if the experience of the youngster's adolescence reactivates unresolved emotional conflicts in the parents personal history. This is the totality of experiences that begins in early childhood through the various developmental stages that every human being travels with before becoming, in turn, a parent.

From a technical point of view, in many cases, support of the parental function can be sufficient to unblock disruptive emotional processes and in turn to help the young person recover the path toward a new development. In other cases, working with preadolescents themselves is necessary, while directly or indirectly continuing the work with the parents as well.

With Lorenzo's mother, for example, it was possible to have only one meeting, which appeared to facilitate the understanding of his clinical condition.

Clinical case: Lorenzo

Lorenzo was 14 years old when his mother brought him for a consultation. He often had a fever which prevented him from attending school regularly. There didn't seem to be any organic cause to explain the recurrent fevers. Lorenzo's mother was concerned that he might have to miss the year. Lorenzo's father had been diagnosed with a tumor just as his mother's pregnancy began. From the very beginning of Lorenzo's life he was exposed to the difficulties the parents had to face in order to cope with the father's illness. Lorenzo was often angry with his mother because he was afraid that she wouldn't tell him the whole truth about his father's condition.

During the final period of his life, Lorenzo's father had treatments in the morning, in the afternoon, and he worked at home even if he had a high fever. In the consultation I had with the mother she described how, when the boy got home from primary school, he would put his hand on his dad's forehead to feel how much fever he had. When she said this to me it was as if the words slipped out of her mouth without her realizing their profound meaning, for herself and, above all for Lorenzo. She was struck by this detail as it highlighted a possible identification the child had with his dad. The fact that the mother understood this made it possible for her to help Lorenzo work through the difficult identification with his dead father.

Lorenzo's father, even now, was very present in their discussions. Lorenzo and his mother still frequently asked themselves how he would have behaved on this or that occasion, often speaking of his abilities or joking about his limits. For Lorenzo, at the threshold of puberty, of sexual development and the representation of libidinal and aggressive urges, somatic symptoms seemed to be attached to the lack of working through of a grieving process in which identification with a lost object would not allow him, for the moment, to recognize elements of aggression toward the dad who had left him.

Mario

In other cases, individual or group psychotherapeutic endeavors have been necessary, journeys that required more time and more structured interventions, and these, too, were accompanied by work with the parents.

Mario (11 years old) presented to the pediatric hospital where I work with strong migaines and and adominal pains, both of which don't have any organic cause. Mario spends a lot of time at home, where he does not, however, have a space of his own. He doesn't have his own room but instead has always slept in his mom's bed, and his dad sleeps in another room. When he tried to ask his mom the reason for this situation, she answered evasively, and Mario had the idea that, actually, his parents didn't want to sleep together. He often complained about having "little space"; just as in his internal world, his physical space, too, was very limited. In the room where he slept, he only had a little bedside table, while the rest of the room was taken up by his mom's things. He had the impression that his birth was "a turning point in my mom's life"; it happened when she was forty years old and was no longer expecting to have a baby.

Little reference was made to his father, in contrast; Mario said only that, while growing up, "I always thought I was more like him," especially in his physical aspect and in his "calm and peaceful" character.

The issue of Mario having his own room is very difficult to bring up with his parents as well, because for them it would mean confronting problematic aspects of their relationship. Only with time can they manage to think about the possibility of a dedicated space for their son, both physical and emotional. With this allusion to separation, Mario will be able to let go of his need to express discomfort through his cephalgias, gradually thinking more about his internal conflicts between a part of him that wants his dad and mom to be more connected to each other, and another part that fears their union would exclude him.

Alessandra

Alessandra (11 years old) presented with a constant contracture of the calf which she had for years and no doctor or specialist was ever able to explain. Alessandra's grandparents, her mother's sister and her family have been living near Alessandra's home since she was born. These extended family members always gather at Alessandra's house for lunch and dinner so that everyone eats together. This family habit started when Alessandra's mother had opened her home to her family of origin, preparing food every day for her parents and sister.

At these regular family gatherings Alessandra became the center of everyone's attention, even her aunt's husband's, who had become part of the nuclear famil. When Alessandra was seven years old – a little cousin was born.

It is difficult for Alessandra and her parents to find any time to be alone together, and accepting the situation of the big, undifferentiated family has not been easy even for Alessandra's mom. Alessandra herself has trouble distinguishing herself as a daughter and seeing herself and her parents as a distinct family.

"Since this has been a problem for me, I didn't want it to be one for Alessandra as well," says her mother. In all these years, her mother has not been able to mentally assign meaning to the discomfort suffered by Alessandra, who – since her little cousin became an "invading presence" – often reacts by shutting herself up in her room. While she says these things, the mother recalls having herself been jealous of her own sister.

At our first meeting, Alessandra reports that now her leg troubles her a little less, but when it hurts, the pain is intolerable. She talks about her attempts to be more independent and to go out alone, but she complains that her parents are afraid to let her go out by herself, which at times she tolerates but at other times she rebels against.

In a different session, Alessandra tells me that things are going somewhat better, and that her calf hurts less. She asks herself if that might be because she has changed or because her relationship with her parents has changed.

We talk about a leg that seems to struggle greatly to remain standing, a difficult situation. Now that someone has noticed what she was trying to make understood, the leg can relax. "What do you think it's saying now?" I ask her, and she replies, "Now it doesn't say anything."

Alessandra expresses intense emotion when she talks about herself, about her plan to get away and live alone once she is eighteen. When I tell her she can share this wish for her own space without being afraid that she is bad or that she is doing something bad to someone else, she answers: "I would like them to understand my point of view, my need to separate ."

She thinks that her parents, too, in some way experience her situation – even though they "went halfway around the world to deal with the problem with my

leg" before at last understanding that it was something else: the wish to walk on her own, to complete her journey of adolescent separation, with all the sorrows connected to that – to unblock Alessandra in her process of autonomy.
sensations in the lower extremities – for example

Diana

Diana, aged 15, who was admitted for an asthmatic crisis, is trying to assert her own identity and her wish to separate from her parents, who are very anxious about her physical condition, they are clearly worried about her growing up. Her respiratory symptoms, not confirmed by the asthma test, recur just before a school trip – this time she also has painful sensations in her feet which prevent her from leaving the house. Diana feels confused when her parents wonder with her if there could be a psychological problem, not a physical one, she tells them that her feet have nothing to do with her head. A few reflexology sessions seem to resolve the pain in her feet but severe asthma attacks persist, especially after clashes with her parents: 'it bugs me that they tell me what to do or what to wear, I want to decide but I feel guilty because Mum gest anxious and then I do what they want but I am angry!'. She then corrects herself: 'Actually, when I don't want to do something, I do it anyway, huffing and puffing, I go to my room and I act as if nothing happened, I don't think about it'.In the following months, Diana has two serious asthma attacks, always before school trips or outings. These incidents are downplayed, even if the second attack was very serious, an air ambulance was called.

A course of psychotherapy, over a relatively short period of time, helped Diana with her asthma crises, as if she was finally able to breathe and walk freely. She began to expand and improve the relationship with her peers; she has become more able to establish her own space and defend it from her overprotective and worried parents. Diana's relationship with them still has ups and downs; the difference is that she can now express her thoughts to them without becoming overwhelmed by the anxieties that were probably causing the respiratory symptoms.

A common preadolescent interest

Many will have the experience of observing children and young people who are passionate about film and comic strips with characters from Japanese stories, and who participate in very long narrative games in which a considerable portion of the cards representing characters in those stories present challenges and endless competitions, with growing levels of ability, strength, and power. A less attentive eye might attribute such interest merely to successful commercial marketing; but in actuality, the activities and cultural content of the games that excite young people represent socially shared modalities for coping with the topics and vicissitudes specific to their age group, including the struggle for survival, supremacy, and power, as well as the growth and development of strength and the tools available.

Marina Sapio, speaking of the delicate period of transition between the no-longer-of-childhood and the not-yet-of-adolescence, emphasizes

...the good fortune contained in collecting and playing games with cards portraying monsters that are as fascinating as they are miraculous, with highly variable ways and capacities to attack.... One can make use of the need to give a face to what is internally obscure, a need that is quite typical during this transitional phase. If on the one hand, these preset figures usurp individual abilities to portray their own monsters, they can also facilitate things for those who can't manage to create their own representations, and they have the advantage of being introduced from the outside.[2] (Sapio 2008, p. 14)

For the preadolescent, being able to play "on the same level" with competitors, gradually increasing one's competence, can be achieved as long as one accepts one's own imperfect nature and the re-balancing of childhood omnipotent fantasies that, in the throes of puberty, can reactivate oedipal dynamics with traces of aggression and violence.

In this regard, Blos (1962) found that, in the young boy, "the theme of killing, subduing, humiliating, and exploiting the giant, i.e., phallic female (the archaic mother imago), returned in endless variations" (p. 62), while the topic of not regressively yielding to Mama is alive in the young girl and leads her toward activity and the other sex.

Once the pubertal youngster breaks the continuation of childhood experience, archaic anxieties open the door to latency-period functioning, involving the ego, its functions, and the superego based on parental figures. Incest and parricide become possible representations in the childhood oedipal relationship with the parents; primitive psychic contents find their principal modality of expression in affect and somatic manifestations.

The phase of actual adolescence (Gutton 1996) requires that what happened in the pubertal phase can be worked through, that symbolic castration is accepted, and limits recognized.

The incipient preadolescent representative capacity and the gradual establishment of symbolizing competence require confrontation with these archaic and terrifying themes and their working through, which, if it fails, would entail refusal of what is connected with development, thereby creating a block, a developmental breakdown (Laufer and Laufer 1984). For Gutton (1996), this consists precisely of the failure of the possibility of mentally representing the pubertal youngster, thus compromising integrated development of psyche and soma.

Conclusions

The clinical material and theoretical considerations expressed in this paper emphasize that preadolescence represents a particularly important period in the lives of youngsters and their families, even though expressions of the youngsters' discomfort may be silently evident, often expressed through the body, far from the clamoring of demands for attention seen in other phases of life.

This is something that invites us to keep an attentive eye on this period of growth in which there is a struggle to balance physical changes with emotional life, where these changes have to be integrated into the mental representations that boys and girls have of themselves. This psychic task often supersedes the capacities for working through and for symbolization in a mind still in formation.

In preadolescence, physical maturation that is at times imperious, together with an enormously increased push from the drives, reactivates sexual fantasies and desires for autonomy. These put at risk both the connection with the parents and the emotional balance established during the course of childhood and can give shape to a compromise symptomatology that privileges mobilization of the body.

Only the subsequent development that takes place in actual adolescence will allow new connections with the self and with others to be forged, and the acquisition of cognitive development to take place, in order to cope with pubertal urgencies. Sublimation and symbolization will make it possible to give up immediate drive satisfaction, the reemergence of oedipal dynamics, and the passage from the incestuous genital object to new objects, while attenuation of the severity of the superego will reinforce idealized needs that are more in harmony.

Nosographical concepts of actual neurosis, neurotic conversion, and psychosomatic expression seem to be useful tools with which to organize the symptomatology of preadolescent bodily expression, locating its various expressions according to the method employed by the psychic apparatus to deal with pubertal drive dimensions and the presence, or not, of a capacity for mental representation.

It is in fact the capacity to transform the pubertal drives into mental experiences that orients us, considering conversion as the youngster's ability to express symptoms as a compromise between instinctual desires and normative moral values. Here, actual neurosis is a quantitatively excessive situation that is also linked to the subject's psychic symptoms as the product of emotional dysregulation, often rooted in experiences during early infancy.

In this entire picture, the role assumed by parents is not a secondary one, given that their children's developmental phases, from early childhood on through complete autonomy, require ongoing re-adaptations and developments. For the parents, as well as for the young person, "the exams are never over."

The way in which a person has been able to cope with his own childhood and his own adolescence becomes crucial in confronting parenthood and the adaptations required by the various phases of children's growth – among which the entire adolescent journey is, without a doubt, one of the toughest. But at the same time, it can represent a new opportunity to again take up the threads of one's own not-fully-completed developmental journey. Once this journey has been faced and resolved, not only will obstacles to the children's development be removed, but parents will also be able to provide the necessary psychic containment for their children's development.

If for youngsters, adolescence constitutes a second period of the process of separation individuation that characterizes the early years of life (Mahler et al. 1975) and is a sort of second birth (Pellizzari 2010), then becoming the parents of adolescents often represents "a third period," in which any relational difficulties that arose in the early years of life or over the course of childhood can find new opportunities for recognition and acceptance.

Notes

1 Translation by G. Atkinson.
2 Translation by G. Atkinson.

References

Abbassi, V. (1998). Growth and normal puberty. *Pediatrics*, 102(Suppl. 3):507–511.

Abreu, A. P. & Kaiser, U. B. (2016). Pubertal development and regulation. *Lancet Diabetes & Endocrinology*, 4(3):254–264.

Blos, P. (1962). *On Adolescence: A Psychoanalytic Interpretation.* New York: Free Press.

Brunelli, P., Balzani, L. & Briganti, L. (2006). Il disagio psicologico e la somatizzazione in età evolutiva [Psychological discomfort and somatization in the developmental age]. *Quaderni acp*, 13(2):76–82.

Cahn, R. (1998). *L'adolescente nella psicoanalisi: l'avventura della soggettivazione [The Adolescent in Psychoanalysis: The Adventure of Subjectivization]*. Rome: Borla, 2000.

Cahn, R. (2006). Origini e destini della soggettivazione [Origins and destinies of subjectivization]. In Richard, F. & Wainrib, S. (Eds.), *La soggettivazione [Subjectivization]*. Rome: Borla, 2008.

Cahn, R. (2009). Una vita di lavoro con gli adolescenti [A life of work with adolescents]. In Goisis, P. R. & Bonfiglio, S. (Eds.), *Essere adolescenti oggi [Being Adolescents Today]*. Milano: Quaderni del Centro Milanese di Psicoanalisi Cesare Musatti, 2009.

Cahn, R. (2013). La psicoanalisi alla prova dell'adolescenza [Psychoanalysis tested by adolescence]. In Monniello, G. (Ed.), *L'adolescente e il suo psicoanalista [The Adolescent and His Psychoanalyst]*. Roma: Casa Editrice Astrolabio, 2014.

Campo, J. V. & Fritz, G. (2001). A management model for pediatric somatization. *Psychosomatics*, 42(6):467–476.

Carbone, P. (2009.) *Le ali di Icaro. Capire e prevenire gli incidenti tra i giovani [The Wings of Icarus: Understanding and Preventing Accidents Among Young People]*. Torino: Bollati Boringhieri.

Carbone, P., Ed. (2010). *L'Adolescente prende corpo [The Adolescent Takes Shape]*. Rome: Il pensiero Scientifico Editore.

Casini, E. (2015). *Somatizzazione e adolescenza [Somatization and Adolescence]*. Milan: Franco Angeli.

Cramer, F. (1977). Vicissitues de l'investissment du corps, symptômes de conversion en période pubertaire. *Psichiatrie de l'enfant*, XX:1.

D'Alberton, F. (2004). Disturbi emotivi ad espressione somatica in preadolescenza [Emotional Disturbances with Somatic Expression in Preadolescence]. *Psichiatria dell'infanzia e dell'adolescenza*, 71:127–142.

D'Alberton, F. (2017). Psychoanalysis in hospital: Early adolescence and somatic functional disturbances. *Italian Psychoanalytic Annual*, 11:121–135.

D'Alberton, F. (2018). *Psychoanalytic Work with Children in Hospital,* trans. G. Atkinson. London: Routledge, 2022.

D'Alberton, F. & Scardovi, A. (2021). Children exposed to pornographic images on the Internet: General and specific aspects in a psychoanalytic perspective. *The Psychoanalytic Study of the Child*, 74(1):131–144. https://doi.org/10.1080/00797308.2020.1859277

De Ajuraguerra, J. (1974). *Manuale di psichiatria del bambino [Manual of Child Psychiatry]*. Milan: Masson, 1979.

Fain, M. (1971). Prélude à le vie fantasmatique. *Revue française de psychanalyse*, XXVIII:3–4.

Fonagy, P., Gergely, G., Jurist, E. L. & Target, M. (2002). *Affective Regulation, Mentalization, and the Development of the Self*. New York: Other Press.

Freud, A. (1936). *The Ego and the Mechanisms of Defence.* , London, Routledge, 2018.

Freud, S. (1894). *The neuro-psychoses of defence*. *S. E., 3*.

Freud, S. (1905). *Three Essays on the Theory of Sexuality*. *S. E., 7*.

Giedd, J. N. (2015). The *amazing* teen brain. *Scientific American*, 312(6):32–37.

Grossman, D. (2002). *Soli, insieme. Discorso Di David Grossman a Letterature [Alone, Together: David Grossman's Literature Discussion]*. 21/5/2002 Basilica di Massenzio, Roma. Cfr. https://forum.termometropolitico.it/227311-soli-insieme-di-david-grossman.html

Gutton, P. (1991). *Le pubertaire*. Paris: PUF.

Gutton, P. (1996). *Adolescens*. Paris: PUF.

Gutton, P. (2000). *Psicoterapia e adolescenza [Psychotherapy and Adolescence]*. Rome: Borla Edizioni, 2002.

Gutton, P. (2008). *Il genio adolescente [The Adolescent Genius]*. Rome: Edizioni Magi, 2009.

Gutton, P. (2013). La seduta [The session]. In Monniello, G. (Ed.), *L'adolescente e il suo Psicoanalista [The Adolescent and His Psychoanalyst]*. Rome: Casa Editrice Astrolabio, 2014.

Jeammet, P. (2007). *Psicopatologia dell'adolescenza [The Psychopathology of Adolescence]*. Rome: Borla.

Jensen, F. E. & Nutt, A. E. (2014). The teenage brain. Blackstone Audio.

Kreisler, L. (1981). *Clinica psicosomatica del bambino [Clinical Psychosomatics ofmhe Child]*. Milano: Raffaello Cortina Editore, 1993.

Kuiri-Hänninen, T., Sankilampi, U. & Dunkel, L. (2014). Activation of the hypothalamic-pituitary-gonadal axis in infancy: minipuberty. *Horm. Res. Paediatr.*, 82(2):73–80.

Laufer, M. & Laufer, M. E. (1984). *Adolescence and Developmental Breakdown: A Psychoanalytic View*. London/New York: Routledge, 1995.

Lebovici, S. (1985). L'Isteria nel bambino e nell'adolescente [Hysteria in the child and adolescent]. In Lebovici, S., Diatkine, R. & Soulè, M. (Eds.), *Trattato di psichiatria dell'infanzia e dell'adolescenza [Essays in Child and Adolescent Psychiatry]*. Rome: Edizioni Borla, 1990.

Luyten, P., Van Houdenhove, B., Lemma, A., Target, M. & Fonagy, P. (2012). A mentalization-based approach to the understanding and treatment of functional somatic disorders. *Psychoanalytic Psychotherapy*, 26(2):121–140.

Luyten, P., Van Houdenhove, B., Lemma, A., Target, M., & Fonagy, P. (2013). Vulnerability for functional somatic disorders: a contemporary psychodynamic approach. *Journal of Psychotherapy Integration*, 23(3):250.

Mahler, M. S., Pine F. & Bergman, A. (1975). *The Psychological Birth of the Human Infant: Symbiosis and Individuation*. New York: Basic Books, 2000.

Monniello, G. (2013a). *L'incontro analitico con l'adolescente. Soggettualizzazione e Principio di realtà [The Analytic Encounter with the Adolescent: Subjectivization and the Reality Principle]*. Relazione tenuta al CPB il 6/6/2013.

Monniello, G. (Ed.) (2013b). *L'adolescente e il suo psicoanalista [The Adolescent and His Psychoanalyst]*. Rome: Casa Editrice Astrolabio, 2014.

Parent, A. S., Franssen, D., Fudvoye, J., Gerard, A. & Bourguignon, J. P. (2015). Developmental variations in environmental influences including endocrine disruptors on pubertal timing and neuroendocrine control: revision of human observations and mechanistic insight from rodents. *Frontiers in Neuroendocrinology*, 38:12–36.

Pellizzari, G. (2010). *La seconda nascita. Fenomenologia dell'adolescenza [The Second Birth: The Phenomenology of Adolescence]*. Milan: Franco Angeli.

Piaget, J. (1964). *Lo sviluppo mentale del bambino e altri studi di psicologia [The Child's Mental Development and Other Studies in Psychology]*. Torino: Einaudi, 1967.

Sapio, M. (2008). Tra il non più e il non ancora: l'enigmatica articolazione tra latenza e adolescenza [Between the no-longer and the not-yet: the enigmatic articulation between latency and adolescence]. *Richard the Piggle*, 16:1.

Schulte, I. E. & Petermann, F. (2011). Somatoform disorders: 30 years of debate about criteria!: What about children and adolescents? *Journal of Psychosomatic Research*, 70(3):218–228.

Sirol, F. (1985). I dolori addominali ricorrenti della fanciullezza e dell'adolescenza [Recurrent abdominal pains in youth and adolescence]. In Lebovici, S., Diatkine, R. & Soulè, M. (Eds.), *Trattato di psichiatria dell'infanzia e dell'adolescenza [Essays on Child and Adolescent Psychiatry]*. Rome: Edizioni Borla, 1990.

Sugarman, A. (2017). The transitional phenomena functions of smartphones for adolescents. *Psychoanalytic Study of the Child*, 70(1):135–150.

Chapter 4

Growing up in digital times and the adolescent's experience of being in-a-body

Alessandra Lemma

Introduction

Being an adolescent today is an experience that clinicians and parents alike who were adolescents in pre-digital times will not share. This generation is growing up neither 'online' nor 'offline' but 'onlife' (Floridi, 2018: 1). Digital connectivity, along with different strands of virtuality, are now an integral part of young people's daily lives. The Internet has changed the world in unimaginably positive ways, but it has also introduced new pressures and risks that are especially relevant to what it means to be an adolescent today. The ubiquity of virtual spaces provides the current dominant context within which adolescents also negotiate their sexual and gender identities, most notably through the domestic use of social media and of online pornography.

The adolescent developmental process is kick-started, as it were, by the challenge of how to integrate the pressing, unruly, messy, frightening, and exciting pubertal body into the self-representation. For some adolescents the pressures of puberty may lead them to find ways to circumvent the reality of the body, sometimes wishing to redesign it altogether, which parents can find deeply unsettling, not least when this manifests as a profound dissatisfaction with the natal body, that is, the body 'given' to them by the parents. This can feel like a violent rejection of the parents, as if all traces of them must be quite concretely erased by changing the appearance of the body.

A key difference between pre-digital and digital times is that in our advanced technological culture, the body can readily be transcended rather than accepted as a cornerstone of reality. It can be corrected, transformed, or altogether bypassed. In this chapter I want to focus on the online, virtual world and consider the fate of the body online. More specifically, I will explore how retreat into virtual worlds may be used by some young people as a way of bypassing the psychic implications of being-in-a-body and the related conflicts and anxieties.

The seductions and perils of technological embodiment

In many aspects of our lives, very real progress has been made possible by technological developments. Additionally, from a psychological point of view, virtual

DOI: 10.4324/9781003351184-5

space may in fact be construed as a kind of transitional space that facilitates helpful experimentation with new identities and the imaginary possibilities afforded by it can be used therapeutically (Turkle 1995, 2005; Suler, 2002, 2004; Allison et al., 2006; Dini 2009). It is also the case, however, that the techno-environments of gaming, social media and online pornography are particularly receptive to the projection and acting out of unconscious fantasy. Like all "good" things they may be put to less good use and the latter is my focus in this chapter.

Moreover, because 'onlife' is part of the technologized landscape that is now considered 'normal', this makes it easier, sometimes less conspicuous, for it to be deployed by young people as a refuge away from the demands of the reality of embodiment and its meaning for them. "Playing" or relating in virtual space may then be used to bypass the arduous psychic task required to represent experience, giving way instead to simulation, with the attendant risk that the virtual can replace the real and become more compelling. Parents may be concerned about the time their child spends online, even if the behavior does not meet clinical criteria for an addiction. The cocoon that virtual space can become may be experienced by parents as a door that shuts them out – just as it often feels to the clinician working with the young person who is immersed in life online and who turns away from an invitation to think about what is happening internally by retreating into their phone within the session itself.

The widespread use of internet-enabled technologies and platforms has spurred debate about their potential effects on people's psychological well-being and functioning. However, even after considerable research, an understanding of the fundamental associations between internet technology use and well-being remains elusive, and results of scientific studies on this topic are mixed (Appel et al., 2020; Vuorre & Przybylski, 2024). Multiple factors contribute to internet use disorders including a combination of psychological, social, and environmental factors. Individuals with pre-existing mental health issues, such as depression or anxiety, may be more susceptible to developing internet use disorders as a coping mechanism. Social isolation, peer pressure, and a lack of in-person social connections in an adolescent can contribute to reliance on online interactions and gaming, for example. There is a mixed body of evidence regarding the positive and negative effects of social media usage specifically. Recent reviews have demonstrated only a weak correlation between social media and mental health benefits (Appel et al., 2020). By comparison, the relationship between inordinate social media usage and adverse effects on mental health is significantly stronger (Raudsepp & Kais, 2019; Wheatley & Buglass, 2019), though this is likely to be mediated by pre-existing vulnerabilities that are then amplified by technology.

In keeping with the gist of the research, my own clinical experience makes me skeptical of the view that spending time in virtual reality games or social media per se "causes" psychological problems. Rather, I suggest that it can provide a culturally reinforced and readily accessible vehicle for the enactment of conflicts related to our embodied nature that some vulnerable adolescents are especially primed for given their developmental histories. The compulsive use of gaming or online pornography, for example, is overdetermined, and may be driven by various unconscious conflicts, but my focus in this chapter is restricted to understanding those clinical presentations where its misuse is in the service of managing a disturbing experience of "otherness" that is felt to be concretely located in the body.

An important question is what distinguishes those young people who turn more predominantly to the online medium as a safe retreat from embodied relationships and even more specifically from embodied *sexual* relationships. This requires more research. Based on my observations in the consulting room, I suggest that there is no single developmental pathway or specific psychopathology that can provide reliable answers to this question. However, for those young people who are at risk of struggling with the demands made on the mind by the physical changes of puberty (due to developmental deficits and/or conflicts), the retreat into virtual spaces proves especially compelling because it allows them to manage confusion and distress about the real body by interposing virtual distance between self and other and between their own body and mind.

The online medium is ideally suited to being 'misused' in the service of managing a disturbing experience of otherness that is felt to be concretely located in the body. We can understand this as in part a function of some of the specific features of virtual space,[1] as follows:

1. ***It denies corporeality.*** Virtual space defies history, transience, and indeed the very physicality of the body. It can be used to effectively suspend the history of the subject, and hence the link to the anchor of the past is eroded, especially as it is recorded in the body. Multiple identities can be adopted and discarded at will. We have, effectively, the creation of what Raulet (1991) has referred to as "floating identities." This could conceivably have some constructive uses if a more positive experience of a "new" self in virtual space can be integrated with life "offline" (Turkle, 1995; Allison et al., 2006). But where this kind of integration is not possible, the potential for pathological splitting is considerable.

   The exhilaration of virtual existence and experience comes from the sense of transcendence and liberation from the material and embodied world, even though we remain embodied, but our experience of embodiment is modified when we engage in virtual space. A vivid example of our yearning for this kind of transcendence can be found in James Cameron's film *Avatar,* in which the main protagonist—a paraplegic ex-Marine—regains mobility through his avatar, never to return to his original, irreparably damaged body suspending the limitations and history of the physical body. This presents the individual with the illusion of limitless possibilities.

   An avatar is also the perfect tool for titrating intimacy. Paradoxically, however, because of the illusion of the anonymity afforded by the mask that is the avatar, young people often disclose a great deal about themselves online, far more than they would do normally. Because 'information' is more important than physical proximity in virtual space, interactions online may then leave some vulnerable people feeling unexpectedly very exposed.

2. *It abolishes the reality of difference and separateness*. It achieves this in two ways. First, by promulgating the illusion of a disembodied self, the tyranny of the specular image need not apply in virtual space. Virtual reality promotes the fantasy that, despite differences, we are "all the same really." It is this promise of *sameness* that makes it so compelling for some young people: it bypasses any exposure to an experience of difference, and to the sense of insufficiency we all must find ways of managing in ourselves. In virtual reality, however, the promise of sameness with an ideal (as projected into an avatar, for example) is forever such that the painful awareness of the given body and of bodily separateness may be sidestepped. This process is aided using mimetic defenses and the development of imitative identifications, which are primitive in nature and based on an appropriation of the other through imitation. Such imitations are fantasies of being or becoming the 'other'. The aim is to *become* the ideal, and not simply to strive to *be like* it. This is especially apparent in virtual games in which people can look like and "become" someone else according to their own specifications.

The second way in which the reality of difference and separateness is abolished in virtual space is through circumventing the reality of geographical boundaries. Technology, starting with the advent of print and then telephony, has radically transformed our ways of communicating and our spatio-temporal organization, introducing new forms of relating and hence of acting in the world with others. Through the medium of representation, we can now bring remote events and people near while experiencing them at a remove (Robins & Webster, 1999). This facility may be used constructively to connect with people who are geographically distant. However, it may also be used destructively to undermine a real emotional connection with others who are physically removed thereby making it easier to bully others online which, in turn, can have a devastating impact on the recipient.

With physical presence no longer required to initiate or sustain a relationship, primary body presence is converted into pseudopresence. The reality and, I would argue, the *necessity* of distance and separation (Josipovici, 1986) are replaced by immediate communication bypassing the otherwise painful psychic work required to allow for the mourning of the absent or lost other. Instead, the thrill of speed substitutes for the reality of a real other who can never be fully controlled by the self.

Pre-Internet we inhabited a world that I have characterized as a 3D(esire) world where 'Desire' was followed by 'Delay' and finally 'Delivery' of what we desired (Lemma, 2017). The psychological 'work of desire' rested on the development of a capacity to tolerate waiting and the state of frustration that this would give rise to. By contrast, the digital generation is growing up in a 2D(esire) world. 'Desire' results in immediate 'Delivery' and bypasses altogether the experience of 'Delay'. A key feature of contemporary technologies is that they abolish, or greatly reduce, the experience of resistance to the satisfaction of one's desire. Internal impediments (e.g., shame) as well as external ones are removed or suspended. Speed now reduces the distance between desire and satisfaction: no effort and no waiting. Effectively, the very experience of the cycle of desire has been disintermediated by the online medium. The intermediary of 'delay' is psychologically significant because it is the encounter with delay that makes possible the representation of desire in the mind. Without exposure to the experience of delay or frustration desire loses its 3D shape that would allow for the various dimensions of the experience of desire to be represented in the mind.

3. *It promotes the illusion of interpersonal transparency.* We can enter a world where there are "no zones of disorder or darkness," as Foucault (1980, p. 52) put it. The strangeness and opacity of the other are circumvented because the other is effectively the self's creation. Here the other – who is also disembodied – can be fully known and hence possessed. The case of Sharon below provides an illustration of this process. Parents may be alarmed and feel excluded by the way that the adolescent may develop very intense relationships with online 'friends' they have never met in person.

4. *It alters the relationship between internal and external reality.* By offering an illusion of what is real, virtual space bypasses the need for the psychic work necessary for understanding that inner and outer reality are *linked* rather than being either equated or split off from each other. In the virtual world, the psychic equivalence mode of reality (Fonagy and Target, 1996) dominates, a mode whereby the internal world that is projected into virtual space is seen to correspond to external reality. In virtual space it is easier to blur the boundaries between internal and external worlds, creating the illusion that internal and external reality are isomorphic. In these conditions of existence, there are no limits to what can be imagined and acted out. As the self becomes intoxicated with omnipotence, it loses all contextual referents – of which the body is one – that would otherwise lend meaning to experience. Thinking is attacked: as fantasy and reality collapse into each other, there is no space from which to reflect. Virtual space may thus be seen as providing a psychic reserve within which all wishes are gratified, as reality becomes an irrelevance, and the individual reclaims the infantile illusion of omnipotence.

5. **It weakens superego functioning.** Virtual space operates like a cocoon, with none of the usual referents that might give pause for thought or impose limits on what is possible to do. Because of the anonymity afforded by the Internet, it can invite a disregard for authority. A weakened superego, coupled with the speed of access, the very broad range of images available, and the design-led enticement to search for more images, can quickly facilitate the escalation of people's sexual fantasies and searches for more extreme imagery than that consciously initially imagined to be exciting. The alliance, as it were, with a morally corrupt rather than a benign, watchful conscience, is further reinforced by the fact that because it is possible to delete browsing history, this fosters the illusion that no-one sees, and no-one will ever know (in practice, of course, this is not so because we still leave a digital footprint).

The features of virtual space that I have outlined may become especially salient and compelling for those young people who struggle to adjust to the psychic demands imposed by the reality of the changing body that puberty forces upon them. During adolescence, when the wish to transcend the body is often at its peak for some young people, the desire to be somewhere other than *in* a real body finds a receptive space in virtual worlds where the body is superfluous, and where mastery, control, and the denial of otherness can be exploited. Immersion in cyberspace may then allow the young person to create "synthetic worlds" (Baudrillard, 1986) in which the body can be dispensed with, history is frozen, and thinking is anesthetized, affecting the capacity to manage conflict and pain rooted in reality.

The body in adolescence

The period of adolescence has been described by several authors as involving an identity crisis (Blos, 1967; Erikson, 1968; Briggs, 2002), but this requires some qualification: the psychic process of adolescence typically sets in motion an unsettling review of personal identity that is *rooted in the body*. Whereas at birth the mind may be said to develop from the body, in adolescence the body presents itself forcefully to the attention of the mind. Erections, masturbation, and menstruation intrude into an oasis of relative calm in the physical domain characteristic of the prepubertal stage. For many young people, the experience of an orgasm becomes a focal point around which a sense of reality of the genital can be further organized, accompanied by a sense of volitional control in the seeking of sexual satisfaction.

At the best of times puberty thus initiates a complicated and unsettling internal process: the physical changes that trigger changes in the body image and hence in self-representation are also accompanied by changes in relationships with others, not least with parents – all these changes, in my view, are inextricably linked and impact reciprocally on each other. The demands made by this developmental transition, however, can for some young people be simply too much to bear (Laufer and Laufer, 1984; Bronstein, 2009; Flanders, 2009). For some, this unavoidable development is experienced as "catastrophic" (Bion, 1970). This is even more so where the quality of early relationships has contributed to a fragile, underinvested or felt-to-be less desirable bodily self, or to entrenched splitting such that body parts may have become identified with bad, terrifying internal "objects". In such cases an adolescent's nose or breasts can be experienced as an alien object residing within the body rather than as an integrated part of the body self and there is pressure to alter the surface of the body in order to free oneself internally of the alien object.

For many young people, adolescence is a time when the question of ownership of the body becomes pressing and often is the focus of conflict with parents: is the body felt to belong to the young person or to the parents? In their detailed work on adolescence, Moses and Eglé Laufer (1984) have highlighted the adolescent's need to change relationship to the body as the key task of adolescent development. As a result of the bodily changes due to puberty, the young person must now integrate into his sense of who he is the reality of the mature sexual body. This is inextricably tied to the resurgence of primitive anxieties about dependency and separation from parental figures, and of oedipal conflicts. For parents, this can also be a very challenging time as they revisit their own adolescence and the sexual anxieties or concerns about the body that they had to negotiate.

When there have been deficits in the baby's earliest relationship with the caregiver and their body, this will compromise the child's relationship to his body, and hence to reality. By the time of puberty, the adolescent's fantasies related to his new body can become profoundly disturbing. The young person may fear losing control over the body and mind. This may lead to an experience of the body as a persecutor that must be attacked. It is not just that the young person must manage the reality of a body that can now actualize sexual and aggressive fantasies, both conscious and unconscious. Under the pressure of puberty, the young person who has not established a secure, positive representation of the body in the mind, will struggle to manage the reality of his separate body in relation to the parental couple. Instead, there may be a need to create an idealized body image, which sustains an experience of fusion with the idealized pre-sexual body linked to the mother. It is only when the young person can feel identified with the mother's body that he can reassure himself against the threat posed by separation. This can then result in a disavowal of the reality of the sexual changes and a marked splitting off of the body (Laufer and Laufer, 1984).

I would now like to turn to two case examples to illustrate how immersion in virtual space became a solution to an inner turmoil connected with their experience of being-in-a-body.

Being a no-body: The case of Paul

Paul was almost seventeen when his parents sought help for him privately. They were concerned that he had become withdrawn, spending long periods of time on the internet, primarily playing computer games, but also using social networking sites. They had been very tolerant of this at first because they thought he would soon tire of it, but when he did not, and his time playing games increased, his mother became worried. Paul was an only child. Both his parents were gifted academics who devoted a great deal of time to their research and other interests. They prized independence and had adopted the stance that Paul would "learn from his mistakes," that "reason would triumph". Like them, Paul was very cerebral; schoolwork had always proved easy for him. On meeting him, however, it was clear that he inhabited his body with less ease: he seemed awkward in his movements, his choice of clothes was very conservative and lacked any personal stamp, and his manner was tentative. He sat in my chair on our first meeting, perched on its edge for the whole session, without even taking his coat off on a hot summer day.

When I asked him why he had come, he replied that he did not want to worry his parents. He told me that they thought he worked too hard and did not go out enough with friends. With some difficulty, he was able to tell me that he felt he was not amusing or entertaining like his friends were, and that he was "awkward" in social situations. He did not have a girlfriend and emphasized that he had no interest in having a relationship, but he chatted to a lot of girls on social networking sites. This suited him, he said, but he also added that sometimes he felt lonely – as far as I was concerned, this acknowledgment was the most hopeful statement he had made in this session. He rounded off this discussion with a pithy "I'm a nobody." At this stage, he did not mention his use of the internet.

As the months passed, the sessions developed a clear pattern: he came, he dutifully listened to whatever I said, and he left without making much of an impression on me; indeed, I often found I forgot what he said or what I had said. The first important development took place around the ninth month of our work together, after he had fallen and sustained a cut requiring several stitches. His mother had left me a message to say she was deeply worried, as he had stopped eating, ignored his schoolwork, and now spent all his time on the internet.

He came for his session five days after this incident, looking very downtrodden. At first, he was very silent, and then he offered this dream: "I am walking slowly and as I walk I see a house collapsing. There is dust everywhere and I get covered in this dust. I can't breathe. I fall to the ground and cannot get back up." He gave no associations to the dream, but after a long silence, he volunteered that he was fascinated by images of detonating buildings and that he often searched the internet for these images. He had been gripped by the collapse of the Twin Towers. He was quick to add that his interest in this event was simply in the images of the fallen buildings, reduced to dust. Since the terrorist attacks he had avoided lifts and tall buildings, he said, and he added, "Actually I have always been afraid of buildings collapsing. As a child, I always read about earthquakes … they fascinate me." He then mentioned, almost in passing, that he had fallen.

I said that his fall had deeply unsettled him, as if it had reminded him that he had a body and that a body was like a building: it *could* collapse or explode and be messy, but he was now not dealing with an image of someone else's body or of a building collapsing – it was *his* body. Paul looked away, evidently uncomfortable with my mention of the body, and I commented on this. Paul said that he wished he could forget the body and "have no body." He said he far preferred "being in [his] head." I said that his body seemed like a scary place to be in, so scary that it was preferable to be "a no-body." Paul smiled furtively, as if he recognized my reference to what he had said in our first meeting and, I thought, felt understood.

He then proceeded to tell me for the first time that he had met a girl on one of the social networking sites he visited and had exchanged a lot of e-mails and text messages with her. After months of virtual exchanges, she had upped the ante and suggested that they meet up. It was, interestingly, after this suggestion that he had gone for a walk – "to clear [his] mind," as he put it – and he had crashed into a lamppost, tripped, and fallen. When he saw the blood, he said that he had felt like throwing up, that it disgusted him. He said he had felt as if it was not his body he was seeing or touching.

I said that the thought of meeting this girl in the flesh had been deeply troubling; it had forced him suddenly into having to think about a real relationship—about sex – rather than a relationship he largely controlled in his mind. It was then that Paul told me he had never kissed a girl, let alone had sex, though he knew several of his friends who had. I asked him what he wanted for himself in this respect. He replied that the thought of kissing repulsed him. All he could see was "an exchange of saliva," which disgusted him. When he was exchanging e-mails with the girl, he had told her he wanted to have sex with her, but he had not really meant it. In his fantasy he had imagined long talks with the girl, "perhaps stroking her hair" he said, but it never went beyond this.

He then recalled being a little boy and spending summers in a mountain resort with his mother while his father wrote his books. His mother would read to him and stroke his hair. He became tearful as he told me this. It was the first time he had ever shown any live feeling in the session. I said he so longed to be this little boy, sitting with his mother, enjoying being alone with her and having all her attention. I said that it was this kind of image that he had in his mind as he communicated with this girl, but that as soon as she wanted to transpose their relationship into the real world of real bodies he became terrified.

Paul was silent, and I sensed his discomfort in his body in a very direct way. In my countertransference I became acutely aware of my own physicality and gender. I said I could see that as we spoke together about these things, the real world of real bodies was alive in the room between us and that he felt very unsettled by it, not sure how to relate to me.

Paul's feeling that he was "a nobody" was an apt description of how the denial of the reality of his body – a no-body – was at the root of his emotional and social difficulties and his retreat into cyberspace. As the work progressed, it became clearer that as a young child he had enjoyed an overly close relationship with his mother. She had seemingly felt neglected by her husband's investment in his work and had turned to Paul for comfort. By the time he was twelve, however, she had resumed her career and Paul experienced this as being brutally cast aside. This expulsion coincided with the onset of puberty. This had left Paul profoundly confused about his changing body and the part it played in disrupting this more blissful preoedipal union with his mother. To manage his internal confusion, he had to find ways of bypassing the body.

Online, Paul could indulge once more in his fantasies of an uninterrupted closeness with a woman/mother. He could even write about sex without this posing a problem, at least until he was taken at his word. Then he literally crashed into something, tripped, and fell, and the sight of blood coming from his body was deeply disturbing to him. I thought that the "crashing" into the lamppost, followed by his falling and the sight of blood, evoked his fantasy of sexual intercourse as a bloody exchange of fluids that disgusted him. Indeed, he told me in a subsequent session that he had "felt sick" when one of his friends had told him about "the blood when you have sex with a virgin."

Paul's preoccupation with, and excitement about, detonating, collapsing buildings could be read in a number of ways, of course. His aggression and fear of the damage he could cause are evident. The buildings seemed to me to be a powerful metaphor for the maternal body – that fantasized house in which he lived tied to his mother, a house forever threatened with collapse by the father – the so-called oedipal rival – and by his own hatred and attacks on the body that he felt had so brutally expelled him. The sexual imagery conjured up by the detonated building will be apparent: it was evidently exciting to him, and yet these images (actual or in his mind) were never used to masturbate, since Paul could not allow himself to do this. Even so, we were able over time to understand how his search for these images reflected his preoccupation with his sexual body – a body he feared and that he experienced as proof that he had lost his mother forever.

A virtual body floating in psychotic space: The case of Sharon

Sharon was seventeen when I first met her. She had been referred to a public mental health clinic because she hated her appearance and was impaired in several aspects of functioning. On presentation, she met the diagnostic criteria for Body Dysmorphic Disorder and was severely depressed.

Sharon came from a relatively deprived socioeconomic background. She was the eldest of two. Her parents lived together, but their relationship was a violent one. Sharon said she hated her father. She felt closer to her mother, even though she experienced her as very inaccessible. The mother was often home, but like her daughter, she was severely depressed.

Sharon described feeling ugly for as long as she could remember, but this feeling took hold in a particularly vicious manner around the age of thirteen. Menstruation had felt deeply unsettling, and she had hated this moment in her life. Around this same time, she said, her face had erupted in acne. Since then, she had been especially concerned about her skin and the shape of her face. Her skin, she said, was now still blotchy and uneven. She could not say what was wrong with her face except that it was the "wrong shape," that somehow it was "too big." She was, in fact, an attractive girl with exceptionally smooth skin, as far as I could see. Yet she spent several hours every morning applying makeup and changing in and out of various outfits before she felt able to leave the house, which was not often. This led her to drop out of college and to disengage from her peer group.

She spent long periods of time at home, lying in bed, playing games on a small Nintendo, visiting online chat rooms, or immersing herself (often for seven hours or more) in a range of virtual games on her computer, where she acquired a new identity and new friends—in short, a new life. She created different characters and was especially concerned with their physical presentation. When she discussed this in therapy, it was clear she felt relieved and comforted by the transformations she underwent in her mind as she identified with her avatars, especially because she could imagine herself in a different and more desirable body.

It was hard to think with Sharon about her use of virtual spaces. She dismissed what I said as irrelevant; the games were "just a bit of fun." The relationship Sharon developed with the computer itself was also important and similarly hard to think about. Interestingly, she was very possessive of the computer. Since she had to share it with the whole family, not least with her brother, access to it was often a source of heated rows. She described to me the way she enjoyed the feel of the mouse in her hand, and the pleasure she gained when she clicked and saw things happen on the screen, as if the responsiveness of the screen to her touch evoked a feeling of fusion with, and hence control over, the maternal object that the computer, I thought, and the privileged space it gave her access to, had become identified with in her mind.

Her description of online relationships was revealing. Once she rather excitedly told me about a girl with whom she regularly "chatted," but whom she had never met: "I know everything about her—I even know when she goes to the toilet!" This statement provides an important insight into one of the appeals of this kind of relationship: this disembodied other, about whom she paradoxically knew intimate physical details, was felt to be entirely transparent, knowable, and accessible. For Sharon, this encapsulated the idealized, fused relationship she wanted to create with her mother. It expressed, I thought, the fantasy of getting right inside her body (she would even know her bowel movements).

Sometimes Sharon missed sessions because she had been on the computer and "forgot."- a scenario that will be only too familiar to parents. When we would explore this, it became clear that she had been immersed in one of the games. When she was playing or online, she entered a state of mind that was completely disconnected from reality: time ceased to matter, and "real" others ceased to exist. She felt very involved in her games and hated intrusions into this idealized space: she responded angrily if either of her parents interrupted her and asked her to do something. She also felt angry with me for intruding into this space through my invitations to think with her about how she used cyberspace. Parents often describe to me their attempts to reclaim their child from the grip of online space and how this is often met with considerable resistance and anger.

Sharon sometimes brought dreams, and it was through these that we were able, painstakingly and over time, to begin to understand the encumbrance that was her body, and the way in which cyberspace allowed her to escape from the reality of her embodied self. I will illustrate this with clinical material over several weeks taken from the end of our first year of work together.

After missing two weeks of therapy because she had felt so low, she had seldom left the house, Sharon arrived for her session irritable. She told me that she had had enough of therapy, that it wasn't helping, and that it was, to use her words, "a waste of time." She said that talking and looking at her dreams was not giving her any practical help. She had come only because she wanted to tell me that she was going to end the therapy. And yet as I listened to her, I sensed that she had come because she was desperate.

I said that even though she had told me that talking and looking at her dreams had been unhelpful, I thought that she had nevertheless made the effort to come because she knew she was in trouble and wanted me to help her stay in therapy. She remained immobile and silent for several minutes and then, as if in a trancelike state, told me of the dream she had the night before: "I am in a dark cave and can't see anything. I try to get out, but my body keeps bumping into hard things and I can feel blood gushing out of my leg. I felt sick and tired, and I curled up in a corner hoping I would die."

I said that she was in a lot of pain and that she wanted me to know this and help shed some light on what was making her feel so bad. Sharon rolled up the sleeve of her cardigan and showed me some superficial cuts, as well as a new tattoo she had done the previous week – her only excursion out of the house. She said, without affect, and as she looked at her arm, "It is painful … I guess."

I said that her body bore the marks of the pain she felt inside and that perhaps, as in her dream, she hoped that if her body died, the pain would stop. Sharon replied that she hated her body and that she had spent the last two weeks wishing she were dead. She had only managed, she said, because she played a lot of computer games and that had taken her mind "off it."

I replied that coming to see me must feel like having to switch thinking back "on" and that this felt like me asking a lot of her. Sharon replied that she thought she was beyond help. I said that being in her body felt like being trapped in a dark cave she cannot escape from. She nodded and said she hated her body. I observed that when she played her games, she could forget about her body. She nodded and said it was "like being someone else … being free…. Claire [one of her avatars] is so cool … she's pretty and smart and no one messes her about."

The next session was a particularly tumultuous one because her computer had broken down that week and she had not been able to access her games for several days except on her Nintendo, which was not the same.[2] She was restless and highly irritable, impatient with my attempts to relate to her. She came across as less articulate than was usual for her; she was confused and struggling to form thoughts. I thought she had decompensated markedly in the intervening week, as if the loss of access to her virtual world had disoriented her, exposing her brutally to a real world she could barely relate to or think about.

She eventually told me that she had felt very "bored" and that she hated not having something to do with her time. I put to her that perhaps she was feeling confused and frightened, which she called "bored." At this point her more dismissive facade gave way, and she quickly became distressed, telling me that she had missed an interview to explore a place at a college (she had forgotten about it), and that her father had told her he would no longer support her, that she had to go out to work. She told me that she was not able to work, that she could not manage this. She then described in detail how unwell she had also been feeling, gripped by a gastric virus that had caused diarrhea: "I was out buying some gum and I thought I was going to lose it and shit everywhere," she told me.

I said that she was letting me see just how dangerous it felt when she lost access to the only space in which she was relieved of this body that kept pulling her down: without that escape she feared that all her messy, shitty, feelings would leak out everywhere. She nodded and said that it had all been made worse by waking up that morning to find her bedsheets soaked in blood.

At her worst, Sharon so disregarded the reality of her body that her menstrual cycle could catch her by surprise, as it had evidently done the night before. She told me that her mother had gotten very upset about this and had shouted at her. Her father had taken one look and told her she "disgusted" him. As she related this, she sounded fragile and humiliated.

I became acutely aware of the physical, visual relationship between us. I said that she was bringing this powerful image of her bloodstained sheets as proof of just how difficult it was to escape this hated body, that somehow it always inevitably left its mark, exposing her to the harsh, critical glare of others including, now, my eyes that perhaps left her feeling exposed in my presence.

Sharon sat back in the chair and pinched the skin on her face: "I hate this," she said, and then pulled out of her coat pocket the Nintendo she often carried around with her. I said she had brought a lot of painful feelings today and that she was now retreating into the safe, predictable world of her games. Despite numerous attempts on my part to reach her, Sharon remained glued to her Nintendo until the end of the session. But watching her was in itself instructive: she tapped away furiously, engrossed in the activity, seemingly confident in her dexterity, and ultimately triumphant as she scored against feeling. I was left feeling redundant as I witnessed firsthand the seduction of the certainty that the machine afforded her and that pulled her away from real interaction with me.

It was clear that my attempt to take up the transference with her had not relieved her; rather, it seemed to turn me precisely into the kind of harsh, critical object she anticipated. As she shut me out, I felt peculiarly exposed and became acutely aware of myself in my own body and very uncomfortable in it, as if I had now become identified with her felt-to-be-physically-repulsive self and it was she who could now ignore me.

These excerpts are very representative of the first year of our work together. They illustrate the pain of thinking, the disturbing nature of being-in-a-body, and the hopelessness Sharon felt in relation to her predicament: "nothing can change." Faced with this feeling, virtual space was a welcoming haven in which she could manipulate her world and her self-representation at will. They also speak to some of the challenges that parents face with their adolescent children. The adolescent's rapid shift from being an irritable, grumpy adolescent to a more fragile, collapsed state can be very hard for parents to manage. The projection into the parents of painful feelings that the young person urgently needs to evacuate can leave parents struggling with being the ones who are excluded or not good enough, for example.

For Sharon, the body was an obstacle that had to be constantly managed and triumphed over, typically through its denial and the consequent retreat into the safe cocoon provided by cyberspace—the computer and the space it linked her into became quite literally a kind of life-support machine; that is, it supported Sharon in managing the demands of reality by providing an alternative to it. The images in her second dream of her "floating" and feeling "light" aptly capture the absence of a body weighing her down and rooting her in the hard reality that, by contrast, she painfully bumps into in the "dark cave" of the first dream.

The image of the life-support machine is especially relevant to this discussion since it captures another feature of virtual space, I would like to draw attention to, namely, the way in which the relationship to the computer, and the space it gives access to, parallels the wished for pre-oedipal relationship to a receptive, desiring maternal body that can be fully known and controlled. The computer's responsiveness could be understood as giving Sharon access to a good "screen mother" – always there, except when it breaks down and then Sharon is once again "dropped." She feels enraged and then frightened, and her capacity to respond to the cues from her real body is severely undermined.

Sharon evidently experienced herself as profoundly undesirable, in her mother's eyes in particular, which she felt more drawn to her brother, but her father's eyes were also unavailable to her. Her body was felt to be messy, disgusting, always leaking and exposing her to the critical eyes of the object. She tried to counter this experience by searching for an alternative, more desirable image of her body through her made-up self in a virtual world, or through her fantasies of cosmetic surgery. These simulated versions of herself allowed her to temporarily create a connection to a fantasized responsive, desiring maternal body. I want to stress, too, the relationship to the computer itself, because as Sharon related it to me, and as I witnessed for myself in the session when she played with the Nintendo, the physicality of the machine and the way it almost molded into her body – and became an extension of it – powerfully reinforced the fantasy of control/fusion with the maternal object/body with which it had become identified.

As will be clear, Sharon was a very depressed young girl who was on the edge of, or in, a psychotic state of mind much of the time. Being online provided her with an extension of the psychotic space into which she retreated in her mind. In this kind of space, the reality of the real world was disavowed, and the quality of Sharon's painful experience was reduced to a kind of intoxication with the virtual promise of a disembodied self and other whom she could access when she wished. When she could not access this state of mind, she effectively broke down as the reality of the body violently intruded (as in her menstrual cycle soiling the sheets).

Conclusion

The delicate and intricate processes that support the establishment of a secure sense of self confidently rooted in the body, and the capacity to reflect on experience rather than enact it on and through the body, may be undermined by the relentless emphasis on transformation, change, and triumph over the body now made possible by a staggering range of new technologies. I have suggested not that these external trends cause new forms of psychopathology, but rather that they may have an adverse impact on the course of the adolescent process in vulnerable young people, and more specifically on the young person's capacity to integrate the reality of the body into the self-representation.

Faced with the external complexity of the demands of the modern world (especially on young people), and the internal complexity and pain inherent in what is psychically required to develop a body and mind that feel one's own, it is tempting to retreat into virtual spaces where the reality of the body is either denied altogether, or where the body becomes solely an instrument for personal gratification, reassurance, and comfort, not the basis for a connectedness with others. For young people like Sharon and Paul, immersion in virtual reality becomes psychically *necessary* in order to control an otherwise disturbing otherness that resides in the body.

Notes

1 There is a degree of inevitable overlap between some of these features.
2 This was due probably to the fact that console games like Super Mario Brothers limit the user's control of the avatar. For example, the player cannot decide how Mario looks.

References

Allison, S., Von Wahide, L., Shockley, T., & Gabbard, G. (2006). The development of the self in the era of the internet and role-playing fantasy games. *American Journal of Psychiatry* 163: 381–385.

Appel, M., Marker, C., & Gnambs, T. (2020). Are social media ruining our lives? A review of meta-analytic evidence. *Review of General Psychology* 24: 60–74.

Baudrillard, J. (1986). *America*, transl. C. Turner. London: Verso, 1988.

Bion, W. (1970). *Attention and Interpretation*. London: Maresfield, 1993.

Blos, P. (1967). The second individuation process of adolescence. *Psychoanalytic Study of the Child* 22: 162–186.

Briggs, S. (2002). *Working with Adolescents: A Contemporary Psychodynamic Approach*. London: Palgrave.

Bronstein, C. (2009). Negotiating development: Corporeal reality and unconscious phantasy in adolescence. *Bulletin of the British Psychoanalytical Society* 45(1): 17–26.

Dini, K., (2009), Internet interaction: the effect on patient lives and analytic process. *Journal of the American psychoanalytic Association*, 57 (4): 979–988.

Erikson, E. (1968). *Identity*. London: Faber.

Flanders, S. (2009). On the concept of adolescent breakdown. *Bulletin of the British Psychoanalytical Society* 45(1): 27–34.

Floridi, L. (2018). Soft ethics and the governance of the digital. *Philosophy & Technology* 31: 1–8.

Fonagy, P., & Target, M. (1996). Playing with reality: I. Theory of mind and the normal development of psychic reality. *International Journal of Psychoanalysis* 77: 217–233.

Foucault, M. (1980). *Power/Knowledge: Selected Interviews and Other Writings*, transl. C. Gordon, L. Marshall, J. Mepham, & K. Soper. New York: Pantheon.

Josipovici, G. (1986). *Touch*. New Haven: Yale University Press.

Laufer, M. (1968). The body image, the function of masturbation and adolescence: Problems of the ownership of the body. *Psychoanalytic Study of the Child* 23: 114–137.

Laufer, M., & Laufer, M.E. (1984). *Adolescence and Developmental Breakdown: A Psychoanalytic View*. New Haven: Yale University Press.

Lemma, A. (2017). *The Digital Age on the Couch*. London: Routledge.

Meltzer, D. (1967). Identification and socialization in adolescents. *Contemporary Psychoanalysis* 3: 96–103.

Raudsepp, L., & Kais, K. (2019). Longitudinal association between problematic social media use and depressive symptoms in adolescent girls. *Preventative Medicine Reports* 15: 100925.

Raulet, G. (1991). The new utopia: Communication technologies. *Telos* 87: 39–58.

Robins, K., & Webster, S. (1999). *Times of Techno-Culture: From the Information Society to the Virtual Life*. London: Routledge.

Suler, J. (2002). Identity management in cyberspace. *Journal of Applied Psychoanalytic Studies* 4: 455–460.

Suler, J. (2004). Computer and cyberspace "addiction." *International Journal of Applied Psychoanalytic Studies* 1: 359–362.

Turkle, S. (1995). *Life on the Screen: Identity in the Age of the Internet*. New York: Touchstone.

Turkle, S. (2005). *The Second Self: Computers and the Human Spirit*. Cambridge: MIT Press.

Vuorre, M., & Przybylski, A. K. (2024). A multiverse analysis of the associations between Internet use and well-being. *Technology, Mind, and Behavior* 5(2: Summer 2024). https://doi.org/10.1037/tmb0000127

Wheatley, D., & Buglass, S. (2019). Social network engagement and subjective well-being: A life course perspective. *The British Journal of Sociology* 70(5), 1971–1995.

Chapter 5

Leaving the shallow end for deeper waters

Collaborative work with parents and adolescents

Jude Piercey

Introduction

The onset of puberty poses important challenges to young people as well as to their parents. An analogy that comes to mind is of swimming from the shallow end to the deep end of a pool. Both parents and children can feel overwhelmed by the changes that accompany this stage of development. Not all children welcome these changes, and it can often be a time of regression, which must be understood within the family context. The aim of this chapter is to show the importance of providing psychological support to the parents alongside the therapy undertaken by their son/daughter. Working with parents collaboratively and consistently not only facilitates the therapy of the young person but it can considerably improve the parent-child relationship.

The onset of puberty and adolescence

Lauren, aged , was referred to me due to her "bad language," aggression towards her mother, and "ritualistic" behaviours. During one session, she broke down and said, "I just don't like this hair growing everywhere on my body. I don't want to change from wearing vests to a bra. I want to stay the same." She insisted on wearing the same jacket every time she left the house, even under her school uniform. Her need for sameness caused significant frustration to her parents.

Lauren was clearly disturbed by the onset of puberty by the looming prospect of high school. The process of finding one's new place in the world involves both internal psychological adjustments and interpersonal challenges.

Neurologically, there are significant changes; chemically, there is an increase in dopamine, a neurotransmitter in the prefrontal cortex that organizes thinking and controls impulses (Weinberger et al., 2005). These hormonal and chemical changes create new emotional experiences that can make both the child and the parents feel out of their depth. I believe the onset of puberty is often the second most significant life-changing event a child experiences, after birth itself. As Bick (1968) describes, being born can feel like being flung into space from the cozy womb, unsure of where one will land. Puberty can feel quite similar.

DOI: 10.4324/9781003351184-6

Collaborative parent work with adolescents

Parent work with these pubescent young people follows a similar path to that described in working with adolescents. However, it is crucial to recognize that this is when adolescence truly begins, and feelings of sexuality, aggression, and the need for independence must now be integrated into a new sense of self. Parents need to understand their child's unique position amidst the "onslaught" of these changes to their minds and bodies.

We need to 'tread water' before we venture into the deep end. As parents, we need to slowly work with our children and all learn together in the therapy – accepting, thinking, holding and containing the child's internal changes and what that brings up for them.

This chapter highlights the importance of working with parents collaboratively when undertaking therapy with an adolescent or pubescent child. Many books have been written about parent work, but often, psychotherapists only conduct periodic reviews with parents rather than working with them collaboratively and continuously. The chapter aims to demonstrate the improved quality of psychological development that occurs when both the young person and their parents are supported simultaneously. It also illustrates the transition from seeing the child as "difficult" to understanding the underlying meanings behind their behaviour.

Research supporting collaborative work with parents and psychotherapy

Research supports collaborative work with parents alongside psychotherapy as an effective treatment method. Weaving the parents' past and present experiences together, as suggested in "Angels in the Nursery" (Lieberman, 1982), through collaborative parenting sessions allows beneficial intergenerational experiences to surface. Fraiberg et al. (1975) introduced the metaphor "ghosts in the nursery" to describe how parents may unknowingly re-enact their own early experiences of helplessness and fear with their children, perpetuating maltreatment from one generation to the next. Lieberman (2005) and her colleagues have shown the value of uncovering the "angels" within parents, growth-promoting, forces that encourage positive emotional development in traumatized parents.

By uncovering and developing parents' capacity to understand, accept, and love their child, the child, in turn, develops a core sense of security and self-worth. For example, during a parental session, after the therapist supported the father's strengths, he said, "I never really understood how I could be important to my daughter." This insight allowed him to reconsider his childhood experiences and change how he related to his daughter, fostering a deeper connection with her.

Barrows (2008) describes parent work as a means to enhance "reflective self-functioning," which positively impacts parents' ability to relate to their children. This process aligns with Fraiberg's view that harmful "ghosts" from the past need not be passed on to the next generation if parents can reflect within a "contained" therapeutic space, offering their children a different experience than they had themselves.

Midgley et al. (2009) provide evidence that supporting and including parents is an essential aspect of psychodynamic psychotherapy for children and adolescents. Parent work helps reduce the risk of therapy breaking down (Novick and Novick, 2011). Holmes' survey of parent work (2018) suggests that current parent work, which focuses on parents' unique personalities, helps parents feel less anxious, think about their child's emotions, and differentiate their feelings from those of their child.

Neuroscience and emotional development

Neuroscience research has confirmed that, from conception, the child's emotional self is sculpted by emotional experiences with the parents (Quatman, 2015). The infant's emotional brain is continually being made "more or less sensitive to neuro-transmissions." This suggests that the human brain wires itself in a certain way due to its interactions with others. In other words, the child's experience-trained emotional brain constantly provides the foundational affective data for their encounter with the social world (Panksepp & Biven, 2012). For example, the child in this clinical case, at the age of 17, is not consciously interested in intimate relationships with members of either sex.

Psychotherapy has been shown to ignite the processes necessary to open pathways in the mind that had previously remained undeveloped or shut down due to overload. This new knowledge of the brain shows that psychotherapy changes the brain's structure, reflected in the different emotional experiences of previously firmly held convictions (Panksepp & Biven, 2012). In conclusion, the research suggests that collaborative work with parents brings the possibility of changing maladaptive patterns of relating in both the child and the parents.

Initial meeting with parents: Moving beyond symptoms

Initially, parents often arrive worried about their adolescent's symptoms, which they perceive as specific to that adolescent. The first therapeutic task is to help the parents move from focusing solely on the adolescent's symptoms to beginning a process of observing and narrating step-by-step interactions of the adolescent relating to others, both inside and outside the family. This process is similar to that of the infant observation seminar leader helping participants increase their capacity to observe interaction processes using their countertransference experiences to enrich their observations.

Meeting the parents before meeting the adolescent provides an opportunity for the parents to spontaneously narrate their story, sharing their feelings about the current family situation and their adolescent. As the parents speak with the therapist, an attempt is made to identify with each parent's anxieties and empathize with what they are experiencing. The therapist listens carefully to their tone of voice, their affection for their child, and their annoyance with their child to discover their ability to see the world from their child's point of view.

In a therapeutic consultation, the goal is to help the parents move from feeling persecuted by the adolescent's symptoms and by the therapist's comments, to gradually becoming more confident in observing interactions and feelings within themselves and their child. It is particularly important to assist parents in focusing on "What do you think your adolescent is feeling and thinking at that moment, and how does that make you feel in response?"

The kind of collaborative work with parents that I am going to illustrate needs to be an integral part of providing individual psychotherapy for a child or adolescent. With each family one needs to consider whether the work with parents is most appropriately undertaken by the individual psychotherapist or by a supportive colleague.

The couple's relationship with one another and the therapist

Simultaneously, the therapist also needs to be very attentive to how parents listen to each other, how they mutually empathize, even if they are separated freely they are able to talk to the therapist and to each other. In this exploratory phase, the therapist notes how the parents respond to attempts to understand the current feelings and anxieties within their relationship with the child and the therapist. Paramount is whether both maternal and paternal functions are shared by each partner in relation to the child.

Why now?

In light of what has been seen, "Why is the referral taking place now?" is a crucial question. When an adolescent's problem has been ongoing for some time, there are often increased parental conflicts that prompt the referral. Alongside this can be the question, "When each of you was your child's age, what was happening between you and other family members?"

Structure, nurture, and development in the family and in the therapy

Family life and developing the "Collaborative Cradle of Concern" with parents requires structure, nurture, and development.

- **Structure:** An attempt is made to provide a setting with as much predictability and reliability as possible. The certainty of having a structured schedule for sessions, with a reliable and empathetic therapist, enables the couple to explore their innermost difficulties safely. Based on their upbringing, each parent brings a unique parenting style that must be harmonized with the other partner's style.

- **Nurture:** Nurture is given to the adolescent in the parents by listening and noting their inner feelings about their child as they narrate their stories. As the parents feel deeply understood, there is a development of their maternal functions of being receptive, nurturing, and more relationally oriented to their child (Rustin, 2009). There is also an enhancement of their paternal functions, including being a separating third, a facilitator of mental structures, and a capacity to manage affect, particularly aggression, and provide psychic safety by demonstrating firm limit-setting (Davies, 2015).

It is crucial to understand and acknowledge the origins of certain maladaptive approaches parents use with their child. Supervision can help the therapist understand the countertransference, including unexpressed family feelings that have been projected onto the therapist. For example, when the family denies a sense of inadequacy, hurt, or hostility, the therapist may feel devalued and negatively critical of the parenting.

- **Development:** It is essential to assess the development of the therapist's and parents' therapeutic understanding. This involves:
    o Helping the parents observe the child's feelings projected onto them as part of the child's unsymbolized or denied emotions and prompting them to think about these difficult emotions (Copley, 2000).
    o Fostering a capacity to observe and appreciate their child's behavior, social conversations, and activities as meaningful mediums through which the young person expresses and works through feelings and anxieties related to family life.
    o Establishing a supportive link between the parents and between the parents and the adolescent that:
      - Fosters love
      - Acknowledges hostility
      - Provides security to bear the unbearable truths of their experiences and behaviour.

The therapist's development

An example of Collaborative Work with Parents: Thinking about the development of the adolescent

Clare, aged 16, was referred for therapy due to concerns from her parents. Her mother was worried about Clare's "distancing" from the family, her angry outbursts, and periods of seeming absence. Father believed Clare was "overindulged" by her mother and that this was the core issue. He described the family as wealthy and felt Clare had been "spoiled" from birth. Both parents wanted her to start therapy, but while the father was open to it, the mother was more resistant, displaying anxiety during the initial meeting.

They felt Clare was very different from their other child and was "spoiling" an otherwise "happy family." Although the parents were critical of Clare, it seemed they felt persecuted by her increasing desire to become separate, which they perceived as adolescence turning her into someone they didn't recognize. This frightened the mother and frustrated the father. Clare's perceived defiance of their authority, such as constantly provoking her sibling and shouting without apparent cause, left them feeling they were failing and not understanding why.

Mother wanted a few quick sessions to put her daughter back on the right path or "swimming in the right lane", because her nerves couldn't manage much more, while the father was more open to considering this a psychological step in her development. Clare had no one to perceive or compassionately understand her underlying feelings and the impact adolescence was having on her. There was no acknowledgment from the parents that Clare was going through one of the most significant changes since birth. Everyone felt alone.

During the initial assessment, it became clear that the couple approached this issue from very different perspectives. While they denied that any marital conflict would be perceived by the children, there was significant conflict, and they managed it in different ways. The mother seemed highly anxious and needed to control every decision made for and by her daughter, while the father had spent much of his daughter's life traveling.

Father's absences were explained by both parents with the phrase:

"He was never away for more than three weeks at a time, and Clare was very used to these separations."

However, upon meeting Clare, I learned she had yet to spend one of her birthdays with her father. She said this with a rather sad demeanour. I later learned that her mother also often travelled with her father on his trips away. Christmas was the same; he had never spent a Christmas at home during Clare's entire upbringing.

Mother, while wanting to be a good mother to her two children, seemed unable to allow any space between herself and her daughter, who was emerging as a young woman in her own right. Her anxiety led her to need constant contact with her daughter by texting several times a day. She didn't understand her own need and felt Clare was being defiant if she did not reply.

One could use the analogy of Clare learning a different swimming style than her parents – this traumatized her mother, even though it was safe.

"What's so wrong with wanting to know that my daughter is safe?" Mother would ask, looking at me questioningly. There was a sense that Mother was emotionally unstable, beneath all her harsh rules and regulations that she insisted Clare comply with.

Clare's demonstrations of anger and rage, followed by a complete retreat from her family (mainly to her bedroom and her mobile, and later requesting to attend a boarding school in a nearby area), gave the impression that she had been unable to develop the inner capacities and rapport with her parents which would help her bear the frustration of living with her family. The family seemed to be *swimming out of their depth* and was confused and frightened by their emerging adolescent daughter.

Mother agreed to the boarding school idea, while Father coped by being frequently absent. He said he would occasionally text Clare to see how she was doing but expressed that he didn't feel as close to her as he did with his other daughter. They were both in denial about the seriousness of the conflict within their relationship and its effect on the family.

The treatment plan

Clare was offered twice-weekly psychotherapy, while the parents agreed to fortnightly parental sessions, also with me, to understand the meaning of their angry and neglected daughter's interactions with themselves and others (Pozzi-Monzo & Tydeman 2007). Clare appeared in the early sessions to be quite lost, both emotionally and psychically. She lacked an adequate psychic structure and seemed to have little concern as to whether she was with me or anyone else. The blankness of her stare was also disconcerting.

Fairly early on in the work with the parents, it became clear that Clare's start in life could have had a profound effect on Mother's anxiety now. Clare had been born unexpectedly at 31 weeks and had to stay in the NICU for seven to eight weeks before she could come home. Mother described this time as terrifying, she felt totally unable to hold herself steady. Every day when she returned to the unit, she expected to find that her daughter had died. She teared up at this thought, and Father intervened:

Father: "Well, that's all in the past now. Clare is fine; we don't need to dwell on this, do we, Jude?"

Jude: "I'm just wondering, hearing this, if perhaps there are some feelings of unsafety for Clare that have become lodged in you, Mavis (Mother), and her need to be thought about. It would have been an utterly terrifying time and perhaps can help us understand your need to keep checking that Clare is safe at various moments of the night and day."

Mother: "Absolutely. I have never been able to feel she is safe," (she sighed as though there had been a voice to acknowledge her anxiety), "and I never could understand why it's been so different with my younger daughter, whom I just don't have the same intensity of fear with."

The younger daughter had been born at term and had come home with Mother 24 hours later.

I found myself, through these early parental meetings, working toward understanding my own critical feelings and feeling more compassion toward Mother. This helped build a solid relationship between the parents and me, the therapist. Mother felt heard, and the next thing to address was the constant absence of the

Father. This absence had always been present throughout the marriage, and Mother had always felt quite alone with her daughters and child-rearing.

Father, through his own therapy, was trying to understand why he appeared to have one foot "permanently" out the door. It was the same with our parental therapy sessions. He thought it sufficient for one parent to be present, something else we needed to work on. He would quite often cancel at the last moment, and Mother would attend on her own. However, with the therapist holding firmly to the arranged, regular, reliable setting for the parental work, Father, who was committed to his daughter, gradually returned more regularly once he understood his importance in the family.

There were times when he was quite hostile in the parental work, as though he had been prevented from undertaking something more important by attending the sessions, but the "parental cradle" did not "fall down," and he would return more regularly.

The parents tended to deny how their own behaviour could greatly disturb their daughter. They could barely imagine that a difficult event could disturb Clare for a week or so and simply could not envisage longer-term consequences. For example, when Mother found her own emotions very hard to control and would take to her bed for weeks at a time, depressed and anxious, they would say that Clare "hadn't noticed," and even if she had, it had happened a few years ago, and anyway, she was away at boarding school most of the time.

Clare could be very quiet and emotionless in therapy, silently, it seemed, waiting for the session to be over. Clare would take a withdrawn, non-speaking position in therapy. She would say, "When things are too difficult to think about, I just don't think about them."

Closing her mind was her protection, and this often meant keeping me at bay. However, her anger would show itself in different ways, such as by sitting head down in her chair with her school hat in her lap. She would continually, with one thumb, press the top of the hat, indenting it over and over again. It looked like quite a forceful action, and I wondered if she was pushing down all her angry feelings, which never seemed to find an appropriate home.

The method of working with the parents went through various phases: Firstly, they were engaged in observing and identifying with their child; secondly, they began to observe their own interactions and emotional responses to their child, thinking of what the child's projections into them could mean about the child's feelings; and thirdly, once a deeper therapeutic alliance with the therapist occurred, the parents were spontaneously able to associate with their own childhood and see how their own childhood experiences, and experiences of Clare in her early life, might have led to projecting certain inner conflicts onto their relationship with their child.

For example, Mother herself had had a very difficult early childhood, full of rules and lots of anxiety and aggression from her parents. She wanted her children to experience something different but didn't have the internal resources when Clare was born so prematurely to "contain" her baby and her own feelings. She wanted a child she could shower with love and protect from the harsh realities of daily life, and hence became what we would now refer to as a "helicopter parent." Also, amid this and the constant worry that Father would leave the family permanently, she denied to her teenager again and again that there were any marital problems.

For Father, who had been sexually abused during his upbringing and had a mother who didn't believe him when he turned to her, he couldn't believe he would have any real "importance" in his daughter's life, and it seemed his teetering on the doorstep was a reflection of not really knowing where he was wanted or where he belonged.

When I asked Clare what it was like having a father who just came and went all the time, she just looked at me and said, "It is normal for me. It's always been like this. It's not a problem because I'm used to it." After she left, I wondered if she was buying into Mother's fantasy that the children knew nothing of the marital issues. However, in the session following, Clare arrived "quietly," sat in the chair, and tears rolled down her cheeks silently for the whole session. She didn't take any tissues, just allowing her sorrow and young, unprocessed grief to flow, both from her eyes and her nose. It felt like she had found a home that could contain her distress, and later in the session, I spoke to Clare, the "little girl," using a storytelling narrative.

Therapist: "I'm curious about these tears. I'm thinking about a little girl who was worried about starting school without a mum or dad to wave her in or to talk about her worries with. A little Clare who's built a great big metal coat around her to feel safe with a 'no entry' sign on it. It would have been very hard to talk through difficulties during your childhood with the constant change of babysitters and never really understanding when Mum and Dad were coming home."

Clare: began to open her mind to her emotional experiences, as her parents' minds were beginning to open to Clare's and their own. There was, of course, another important opening that needed to happen: the realization that Clare's adulthood wasn't really very far away, and this implied separation and losses for all of them.

During the course of the therapy with Clare and the work with her parents, their perception that Clare's behaviour had meaning changed from seeing her simply as an angry, anxious, removed adolescent to understanding that there was anxiety coupled with hurt and anger underneath her outbursts.

The parents, whilst always expressing to me how much they loved their daughter, felt lost as to how to help her. Mother said she missed the closeness she used to feel with Clare but really couldn't stand being with her very much as she was beginning to feel she was losing control over her adolescent daughter. Clare, herself, was feeling she was losing control over her own body as it was growing and changing, and however "mature" she might appear on the outside, on the inside, it was very different.

The parents gradually became aware of how their own inner conflicts, their "ghosts from the past," interfered with being with their daughter in a helpful way. What was clear is that everyone in the family needed to be heard and understood, and that it was crucial to repair both the parents' and their child's developmental deficits.

Observations as interventions and guides to understanding

Clare wore loose, amorphous clothes to therapy, covering her developing female body. She talked about being the friend everyone turned to with their emotional issues because they found her "very logical," something Clare seemed proud of.

Clare appeared to embrace the role of her peers' "psychological helper," perhaps to avoid dealing with her own emotional distress, displacing it onto others and not allowing herself to experience such feelings. In one session, Clare told me she had to change rooms in the boarding house. She had described her previous room in great detail, explaining how she felt safe there, and she was given only 24 hours' notice to move. When she told me, I sensed the disappointment she didn't allow herself to feel.

With curiosity, I noted to Clare that she seemed unaffected by the frequent changes and "unknowns" both at school and home. Over time, I gently wondered with Clare if other feelings were hidden underneath. I asked her mother how Clare had reacted at home to the news of moving from her beloved room. Her mother said it had been a difficult weekend, with Clare being grumpy for no apparent reason, but she "reassured" me that moving rooms hadn't upset Clare at all. Upon further discussion, her mother became more interested in understanding what might be going on in Clare's mind. She wondered, for example, if something had upset Clare a few days before that she couldn't verbalize at the time.

Conversations between the parents and me became deeper, but I remained mindful of the sensitivities of these parents, who were often "self-blaming." We began to talk about the pain Clare might be feeling internally but had no way of expressing or working through verbally. The parents started to realize that beneath Clare's façade, all was not well.

They began to use the 'Observe, Think, Talk' (OTT) method (Blake, 2008,) in their observations of Clare, taking more time to think about what was happening for her:

- **OBSERVE** – Clare's behaviour
- **THINK** – about what had happened, which could take place just a few minutes after the behaviour, to a couple of days afterwards
- **TALK** – about the behaviour together, to see what they could learn and uncover, discover and work together on.

They began to realize that things did matter to Clare and that she had inner experiences not directly obvious through her controlled, nonverbal expression. They then saw her obsessive control of emotions, like "not minding" and "not having any feelings about relationships" – as indicative of hidden, overwhelming emotional responses to her experiences. Bearing this in mind, her parents began to relate to their daughter differently. Gradually, they acquired a new sense of Clare's internal world as complex, meaningful, and worthy of respect (Sehon, 2018). This, alongside therapy, enabled Clare to advance psychologically.

Her father gradually started to take an interest in Clare's emotional experiences, which helped him understand his own anxiety more deeply. Between sessions, he sent many emails to the therapist, mentioning his observations and reflecting on his previous "amusement" over Clare's anxiety about him leaving the marriage. Clare had expressed that she never wished to have a partner, get married, or have children. He began to wonder if part of him, "always with his foot out the door," had influenced her views on relationships. He acknowledged his anxiety about staying in the family and returned to his therapy to work on these issues. He realized his "pretending" that everything was okay hadn't fooled his daughter. It seemed Clare had two anxious parents, making it difficult for her to feel safe, so she denied herself access to her feelings.

Conclusion

This paper presents a model of collaborative work with parents (Rustin, 1998) that restores and establishes the parent-child relationship as a lifelong positive resource for both (Novick and Novick, 2011, p.17). The following methods are illustrated:

- **Support for parental functioning,** including limit setting, observing, and finding meaning in the child's behaviour (Magagna, 2014). A change in family functioning occurred as the father and mother began working together. This involved the mother turning to the father and finding a way to calm their child rather than shouting at her.
- **Establishing a structured setting** for parental work, which involved gaining trust in the therapist so that deeper emotional experiences could be revealed, explored, and contained by both the therapist and the parents.
- **Fostering parents' skilled analytic observation** alongside the therapist, including analytic listening and careful attunement to the nonverbal communication of both parents and their child.

Often, it is possible for the therapist to also work with the parents. By engaging with both parents and child within this complex, dynamic family system, it was possible to catalyze the development of a "family mind," facilitating the child's psychological development (Pichon-Rivière, 2017).

Bibliography

Bagnini, C. (2012). The Persecution of Divorce. In C. Bagnini (Eds.), *Keeping Couples in Treatment*. Lanham, Maryland: Jason Aronson.

Barrows, P. (2008). The Process of Change in Under-Fives Work. In L. Emanuel & E. Bradley (Eds.), *What Can the Matter Be? Therapeutic Interventions with Parents, Infants, and Young Children*. London: Karnac.

Bick, E. (1968). The Experience of the Skin in Early Object Relations. *International Journal of Psychoanalysis*, 49, 484–486.

Bion, W. R. (1970). *Attention and Interpretation*. London: Maresfield Library.

Blake, P. (2008). *Child and Adolescent Psychotherapy*. IP Communications.

Byng-Hall, B. J. (1995). Resolving Care-Control Conflicts. In *Rewriting Family Scripts*. New York: Guilford Press.

Copley, B. (2000). Family Explorations. In M. Rustin & M. Quagliata (Eds.), *Assessment in Child Psychotherapy*. London: Duckworth.

Daniel R Weinberger, Brita Elverag, Jay N Giedd, The Adolescent Brain, Washington DC: National Campaign to Prevent Teen Pregnancy, 1, 10–12.

Davies, H. (2010). Children Whose Parents are at War. In *The Use of Psychoanalytic Concepts in Therapy with Families*. London: Karnac.

Davies, N. (2015). *The Paternal Function and Its Conceptual and Therapeutic Relevance* PhD Thesis. University of Witwatersrand, South Africa, p. 87.

Fraiberg, S., et al. Ghosts in the Nursery. A psychoanalytic Approach to the Problem of Impaired Infant-Mother Relationship, Journal of American Academy of Child Psychiatry, 1975, 14(3); 387–421.

Freud, S. (1905). Fragment of an Analysis of a Case of Hysteria: The First Dream. *Standard Edition*, 7, 1414.

Freud, S., Strachey, J., & Richards, A. (1991). *Introductory Lectures on Psychoanalysis*. London: Penguin.

Holmes, J. (2018). Aims in Parent Work: A Brief Qualitative Survey of Parent-Centered Work. *Journal of Child Psychotherapy*, 44(2), 1–12.

Kennedy, E. (2003). *Child and Adolescent Psychotherapy: A Systematic Review of Psychoanalytic Approaches*. London: North Central London Strategic Health Authority.

Lieberman, E., Padro, E., Van Horn, P., & Harris, W. W. (1982). Angels in the Nursery: The Intergenerational Transmission of Benevolent Parental Influences. *Psychoanalytic Quarterly*, 51(4), 612–635.

Lieberman, A., Van Horn, P., & Ippen, C. (2005). Towards Evidence-Based Treatment: Child-Parent Psychotherapy with Preschoolers Exposed to Marital Violence. *Journal of the American Academy of Child & Adolescent Psychiatry*, 44(12), 1241–1248.

Lucey, C., Sturge, C., Fellow-White, L., & Reder, P. (2003). What Contact Arrangements Are in a Child's Best Interests? In P. Reder, S. Duncan, & C. Lucey (Eds.), *Studies in the Assessment of Parenting*. Hove, East Sussex: Bruner-Routledge, pp. 267–281.

Lupinaci, M. A., & Zavattini, G. C. (2015). Equilaterality: The Structure of the Couple and the Mental State of the Therapist. In G. C. Zavattini, B. Bianchini, M. Capello, L. Dallanegra, M. A. Lupinacci, F. Monguzzi, & L. Vitalini (Eds.), *Talking with Couples*. London: Karnac.

Midgley, N. (2009). *Child Psychotherapy and Research: New Approaches*. London: Routledge.

Monguzzi, F. (2015). *Le Ferite della Genitorialità*. Milano: FrancoAngeli.

Morgan, M. (2014). The Couple State of Mind and Some Aspects of the Setting in Couple Psychotherapy. In D. E. Scharff & J. S. Scharff (Eds.), *Psychoanalytic Couple Therapy: Foundations of Theory and Practice* (pp. 125–130). London: Karnac.

Novick, K. K., & Novick, J. (2011). *Working with Parents Makes Therapy Work.* New York: Jason Aronson.

Palmer, R., Nascimento, L. N., & Fonagy, P. (2013). The State of the Evidence Base for Psychodynamic Psychotherapy for Children and Adolescents. *Child and Adolescent Psychiatric Clinics of North America*, 22(2), 149–214.

Panksepp, J., Biven, L., (2012) The Archaeology of Mind: the Neuroevolutionary origins of human emotion, W.W. Norton & Company.

Pichon-Riviere, E. (2017). Family Groups: An Operative Approach. In D. E. Scharff, R. Losso, & L. Setton (Eds.), *The Pioneering Work of Enrique Pichon-Riviere*. London: Karnac.

Phillips, A. (2008). *Saying No*. London: Faber and Faber.

Pozzi Monzo, M., & Tydeman, B. (Eds.). (2007). *Innovations in Parent-Infant Psychotherapy*. London: Karnac.

Quatman, T. (2015). *Essential Psychodynamic Psychotherapy: An Acquired Art*. East Sussex: Routledge.

Reich, T. (1948). *Listening with the Third Ear*. New York: Grove.

Rosenfeld, H. (1987). *Impasse and Interpretation*. London: Routledge.

Rustin, M. (1998). Dialogues with Parents. *Journal of Child Psychotherapy*, 24(2), 238–252.

Rustin, M. (2009). Work with Parents. In M. Lanyado & A. Horne (Eds.), *The Handbook of Child and Adolescent Psychotherapy*. London: Routledge.

Scharff, D. (2014). Aggression in Couples. In D. & J. Scharff (Eds.), *Psychoanalytic Couple Therapy*. London: Karnac.

Sehon, C. (2018). Discussion of This Paper in the 2018 International Psychotherapy Conference in Bethesda, Maryland, U.S.A.

Witek, J. (2014). *The Book of Feelings*. New York: Abrams Appleseed.

Chapter 6

Considering concurrent work with parents of adolescent patients

Kerry Kelly Novick and Jack Novick[1]

Introduction

In 1911, Freud said that development in a child can only take place "provided one includes the care it receives from its mother" (p.220). Many years later Winnicott (1965) said that there is no such thing as a baby, there is only a mother and a baby. Between those two psychoanalytic comments and in subsequent years there has been a neglect of the role of parent work in the dynamic treatment of children and adolescents.

We have talked since 1990 about an evolving model of parent work and summarized our views in a book (Novick, K. & Novick, J. 2005) and in papers published and presented subsequently (Novick, J. and Novick, K. 2009, 2011; Novick, K. and Novick, J. 2008). The model asserts that parent work is substantive and legitimate and makes use of the full repertoire of psychoanalytic interventions. Progression through the phases of the child's treatment affects and is dynamically affected by interaction with the parent work. Parental consolidation in the phase of parenthood may also be profoundly impacted by the child's forward developmental movement.

Why work with parents of children and adolescents?

The main reason for working with parents is pragmatic, since we can demonstrate that it helps people enter treatment, stay and do the necessary work, and leave in a timely fashion, maintaining the benefits of the work (Novick, K. and Novick, J. 2005, cf. especially p.167).

Additional reasons are:

- Children continue to live in and will return to their family and environment – treatment gains are more likely to be retained if the family has changed too.
- Parenthood is a phase of development – adaptive growth in parents supports child change; parental pathology destroys child treatment gains.
- Parents are a big part of the child's world, sometimes the best part (E. Furman 1995). They are also part of the child's troubles, either primarily as part of the cause, or secondarily as affected by the impact of disturbance.

DOI: 10.4324/9781003351184-7

- Parents have anxieties specific to each phase of treatment, which can affect maintenance of the treatment and termination.

What are the assumptions underlying our model of parent work?

- Parenthood is a normal adult developmental phase, with subphases that are affected by dynamic interactions with their children (Benedek 1959).
- Parents and children are involved in a life-long complex interaction.
- Growth consists of a series of transformations in children, parents and the relationship between them.
- Development involves epigenetic interactions at all levels of complexity, but foremost in this context are the interactions between child and parents throughout life.
- The "growth of self-regulation is a cornerstone of early childhood development that cuts across all domains of behavior" (National Research Council, Shonkoff and Phillips 2000, p.3).
- The mode of self-regulation can be characterized in terms of two systems of functioning, which we have called "open" and "closed."
- Treatment of children has dual goals
  o *Restoration of the child to the path of progressive development* (A. Freud 1970)
  o *Restoration of the parent-child relationship to a life-long positive resource for both*
- The therapeutic alliance is a conceptual framework for ongoing parent work. It operationalizes the open system of self-regulation.
- Accomplishment of therapeutic alliance tasks promotes attunement.

Recently we have seen an increasing acceptance of the general idea of working with parents of child patients. What remains, however, as an area of controversy, conflict, and resistance, is the question of whether and how much therapists should or can work with the parents of adolescent patients. All of the assumptions relating to parent work that we have listed above apply equally, in our view, to work with adolescent patients and their parents.

We have noted (DeVito, Novick, and Novick 1994, 2000) that most psychoanalytic adolescent therapists and theorists have held definitive views that the goal of adolescence is separation; that normal adolescents need to keep thoughts, wishes and activities secret from parents as part of the separation process; and that adolescents need allies in the inevitable clash of generations, because of a "normal" need to rebel against all authorities. Each of these views has been axiomatic both in child analytic education and indeed in the cultural view of adolescence, and each has influenced technical choices in how adolescent treatments are designed. With this standard concept of adolescent development, parental intrusion and/or the young person's inability to separate are seen as the major obstacles to adolescent treatment and growth. Many analysts who work with adolescents therefore regularly refer parents to another clinician. Questions cluster around how to maintain confidentiality and lead to the even larger issue of conceptualizing the developmental goals of the phase of adolescence.

Our view of adolescence is different. We see the major developmental tasks for both parents and adolescents as involving transformation of the self and the relationship, in the context of separateness rather than separation. If adolescent therapists work from the assumption that the goal of adolescence is transformation, concurrent work with parents and adolescents will move them all into a new level of relationship. Without concomitant change in parents, it is doubly hard for adolescents to progress into adulthood.

We want to emphasize that we are assuming that the center of the treatment plan is the therapeutic work with the individual adolescent. Whatever one's theoretical orientation or theory of technique, the individual treatment is where the young person grows and changes. Concurrent parent work supports and facilitates that effort, and does not substitute for it.

Not every treatment can or should be the same; this is not a prescriptive model or an effort to establish rules for doing analysis. Some young people refuse to let their parents be seen; some parents are disengaged; some parents micro-manage their children's lives; sometimes adolescents and their parents live at great distances, with college attendance far away from home, work or military commitments necessitating absence; contentious divorce or pathology can make teamwork difficult; death or illness can make a parent inaccessible.

What we deem central, however, beyond the practicalities of particular treatment plans, is that analysts keep the parents in mind, hold the parent-child relationship in the world of the treatment. In this chapter, we suggest that much more can be accomplished in adolescent treatment, more quickly and deeply, when the analyst includes this dimension in all aspects of the therapeutic endeavor.

In this chapter, we offer clinical examples from an older adolescent and his parents to illustrate some of the techniques at the outset of treatment that follow from our model of dynamic concurrent parent work throughout the phases of treatment. Using the tasks of the therapeutic alliance as a conceptual framework, we describe initiating the work toward the dual goals of restoration to the path of progressive development and restoration of the parent-child relationship. We pay particular attention to the unfolding of conflicts between closed-system omnipotent functioning and open-system reality mastery, and the role of fathers in late-adolescent development.

From the evaluation and recommendation to the beginning of treatment-kevin

To us, evaluation is a crucial phase of work with a family. There is the effort to encompass the world of the potential patient and his parents; the analyst works to initiate various psychological transformations in the service of assessing capacity for change, discerning areas of strength, as well as resistance or pathology, and creating a therapeutic alliance; the road map and working conditions for a possible treatment are laid down. All this takes time – varying amounts for different families.

Kevin's mother called me[2] to arrange a meeting with her nineteen-year-old son. She said he wasn't interested in therapy, since he thought the problem was all his dad and that his dad should go into therapy. She too thought her husband was troubled, but Kevin was really struggling with serious problems. He was on academic probation and was very depressed. The two antidepressant medications that had been prescribed did not seem to be working. Kevin had not spoken with his father in a whole year.

She was in town from a distant city, helping Kevin move to new lodgings, since he had left his fraternity. Could she have her son call me if he would accept her idea? She thought that he would refuse. I suggested that first we could meet, since she was here now. In that interview she recounted some history of both parents' families and offered her hypothesis that Kevin's troubles stemmed from the father's job loss when Kevin was a young adolescent. As she described the upheaval and disputation in the family business around Father's role, it became clear that everyone was still reverberating. Mother was dealing with tremendous sadness and frustration. I then defined it as a family trauma, which suggested a way to talk with Kevin about coming in.

Rather than telling Kevin he needed therapy, I suggested that she say that she had talked to me about the job loss, the father's subsequent anger and withdrawal, and its impact on everyone. She could say that I had called it a trauma that everyone in the family needed to talk about. It had helped her to talk to me about it, and it might help Kevin too.

Kevin called that afternoon, and I saw him several times over the next few days. He first vented about his father being controlling, demeaning, and blaming. He felt no respect for his father anymore and didn't want to talk with him. I said I could see from what he and his mother had told me why he felt so disappointed and angry. Then I wondered why Kevin was having so much trouble in school and with friends if the problem was all his father's. He told me it was his father's fault, since he had never felt bad before, the way he did at the present time. He talked about his academic difficulties and the isolation and alienation he felt from other kids. He worried that they found him weird, even gross.

It sounded as if he were damaging himself in order to get back at his father. Building on Kevin's interest in politics, I remarked that he was being like a suicide bomber, attacking the enemy by destroying himself. Kevin was very taken with this metaphor. I noted that suicide bombing is a weapon of people who feel helpless. Did Kevin feel so helpless? Was he interested in finding some other way to feel effective?

Over the next week, we continued to meet and talked about finding the strength to explore more adaptive solutions and do without medication. I introduced the idea of emotional muscle, and Kevin found this so intriguing that he called his mother to tell her how useful he was finding the metaphors we were coming up with. She called me to say how encouraged she felt by Kevin's involvement; she hadn't heard him this positive in years. This allowed me to say that Kevin and I had discussed stopping his medication.

Kevin's mother began to talk about therapy, and I agreed that this now seemed a realistic possibility. I said I would talk with Kevin about this. But a treatment plan could not be finalized until I had spoken with her and her husband about the dual goals of treatment and the working arrangements for our collaborative effort. I explained that treatment would aim to restore Kevin's capacity to choose progressive solutions and equally include work to strengthen the parent-child relationship. I asked her to convey this to her husband and said I would like to speak with him soon.

When Kevin and I discussed embarking on a regular analysis, meeting four times a week with the specific goal of finding his strengths, building on them, and transforming his relationship with his parents, I told him that any treatment with him would have to involve his parents as well. He had no objection; Kevin wanted me to talk with his father, since he still believed his father was the source of all his troubles. Kevin wanted treatment for himself, and he retained the wish that I would also treat his father and change him.

Although Kevin expressed no concern about confidentiality, I raised it, emphasizing the distinction between secrecy and privacy. I said that the details of his own story, which we would learn together in various ways, would be kept absolutely private. Thoughts and feelings are private to him, and he would be making the choice whether to share them with me or anyone else. Actions are public; dangerous or potentially dangerous actions don't come into the realm of privacy, and we would work out together what to do in such an instance.

Kevin responded to the discussion of privacy and secrecy by phoning his father, speaking to him for the first time in over a year. All of my contacts to this point had been with the mother, but, following Kevin's phone call, the father joined our next parent meeting. As we talked, the father expressed his gratitude for the change and was impressed that Kevin had taken the initiative to stop his medication. Mother agreed enthusiastically with working arrangements for an analysis, including regular parent phone sessions and occasional meetings when they came to town. Father, although grateful, was still ambivalent and wanted us to work month-to-month. He also had various controlling strictures about fees, payment, and billing statements. These would become issues later but gave me a current reality confirmation of Kevin's description of his father's style.

In our joint phone sessions, both parents talked more about Kevin's history and gave me a vivid picture of what he was like when he was little. I began to hear how much Kevin had looked up to and idealized his father before the family trauma. I could take up with the parents and with Kevin how important their mutual love had been to them all and what a loss they had all experienced. Despite the father's prickly stance, it was clear that he loved his son. This primary parental love was essential knowledge for me in withstanding the times when the father reverted to his bullying style. I was able to stand firm that a month-to-month arrangement would undermine the treatment; on the basis of his underlying wish to do the best for his son, the father could allow me to be in charge of knowing how best to conduct Kevin's treatment.

I encouraged both parents to call or e-mail anytime they had questions or concerns. During the first few weeks of analysis, Kevin's mother called numerous times with worries about Kevin's moods, wondering if he needed her to come. These talks with her helped me discern immediately a dynamic pattern that had not yet appeared in the early sessions with Kevin. I told him each time his mother called and wondered if he was aware that his distress always mobilized her anxiety and made her wish to fly in and rescue him. Fairly soon we established a shorthand vocabulary for such interactions and could spot them as they arose.

As he began to control his need to worry about his mother, he brought this dynamic into the treatment relationship. His mastery of alternative ways to connect with his mother showed in Kevin's humor when we both picked up his whining or being pathetic, and he joked that he had better call his mother, so she would fly in. After six weeks of analysis, when he went home for Thanksgiving, the whole family noted Kevin's changes. They were thrilled to see his increased lightness and engagement. Kevin, however, reported to me that he felt weird, not knowing what to say or how to relate.

This dynamic sequence illustrates the complexity and immediacy of concurrent individual and parent work. Mother first brought the "connection through pain" (J. Novick and K. Novick 2007 [1996], 2016) in her distress. I took this up with Kevin, who then became more aware that this was his way to stay close and have a unique relationship to his mother. Kevin and I worked on this, and I simultaneously talked with both parents about their side of the dynamic. My established good relationship with the mother allowed me to suggest and reinforce other ways of responding to Kevin, but the father became an unexpected ally, as he said he had always worried about her coddling Kevin.

Kevin's experience of emptiness over the November long weekend break pointed the direction for continued work in his analysis on the role pain played in his overall personality and history. We could see that there would be a struggle to set aside this closed-system functioning and discover alternative ways to relate to himself and others. Kevin's analysis was by now well established in the beginning phase. We could of course anticipate intense resistance arising from various sources in Kevin, his mother, and his father at different times.

These early months of Kevin's treatment brought various changes. His parents began to engage in a number of transformations, reworking aspects of their relationship with each other, Kevin and his siblings, and with the events of their shared histories. They no longer felt helpless or needed to externalize responsibility. Their importance as parents of an adolescent was established, and they embraced the dual goals of treatment. They did not feel excluded but respected the privacy of Kevin's analysis.

Kevin moved from a position of holding an unrelenting grudge, from psychic stasis, to beginning a dynamic reworking of his personality structure. He could allow himself to be with his analyst, beginning to engage in joint work. Moving out of a fixed, sadomasochistic stance with each of his parents, Kevin began to relate to them as separate individuals. He began to experience his conflicts inside. All of these gains were enriched and accelerated by the concurrent parent work.

Difficulties in concurrent parent work

The above vignette describes a successful passage through some of the many shoals that can make treatments founder at the outset or end prematurely. But it may not adequately convey either the detailed difficulties of parent work or the impact of parental pathology on the process. Even as we seek to engage the best parts of parents in the endeavor, we have to stay mindful of the darker dimensions of parental hate and destructiveness to children, both individual and cultural (Young-Bruehl 2011), and the potential for parents to sacrifice their children for their own psychic needs or the survival of the marriage.

Parental defenses

It was hard for Kevin's father to begin to question his idealization of his own father's abusive behavior. Only when this dynamic process was set in motion in the parent work could he abate his relentless criticism of Kevin, which in turn created space for Kevin to take responsibility for his self-destructiveness.

Revisiting family history

Difficult or painful events in family histories, like family secrets, can all too easily become a toxic inhibition of forward movement in a treatment. If they go unaddressed, there can be a validation of omnipotent belief that thoughts and feelings are really dangerous. This creates a destructive fault line in the treatment.

Pathological parental interactions

Divorced parents highlight general obstacles to concurrent parent work, such as externalization, refusal to engage, refusal to take responsibility, the use of therapy to maintain their pathological equilibrium, the use of the child for their own needs, and so forth. All of these may be characterized as a negative therapeutic motivation (Novick and Novick [1996], 2007), in which parents bring a child to treatment in order to make it fail. There are also situations where the level of hatred and bitterness is so great that there is no remedy and treatment cannot get started or be maintained.

However, even when the level of acrimony is quite high, we have found ways to implement our model of concurrent parent work. There may have to be an extra effort to point out that parents have not divorced themselves from their important parenting function by maintaining conviction about the dual goals. The task of transforming relationships with two adversarial parents is greater for the young person, especially when parents promote loyalty conflicts. Our model gives therapists room to be creative in structuring the work. One can work with both parents together, with them in separate alternating sessions, by phone, e-mail, or Skype, including the patient or not, and so forth. Flexibility and willingness to meet each family's configuration are crucial.

The developmental point of view

We locate the work described in this paper in both the century-old psychoanalytic tradition and in the capacity of psychoanalysis to continually expand and absorb new findings. Many years ago, Freud (1916) confronted the age-old nature-versus-nurture debate by suggesting a complementary series, where the two are in constant interaction. Erikson elaborated this to formulate an epigenetic series in which development occurs from complex interactions that continue across the life span (1950). The most recent neuroscientific work takes the same position. The Harvard neurobiologist Steven Hyman states, "The old 'nature vs nurture' debate has long receded into scientific irrelevance. Instead, the frontier lies in understanding the mechanisms by which environmental factors … interact with the genome to influence brain development and produce diverse forms of neuroplasticity over the life time" (2009, p. 241).

Each discipline works with a set of assumptions and an epistemological strategy. As psychoanalysts, we assume the following epigenetic developmental fundamentals:

- A developmental approach is a crucial metapsychological dimension of understanding personality functioning.
- The developmental approach is what differentiates psychoanalysis from many other psychological theories.
- A developmental approach assumes that all behavior has meaning and a history.
- Development can only take place in the context of relationships.
- A child's history encompasses generations, at the very least the parents and the beliefs and fantasies they bring to rearing the particular child. Cultural influences are transmitted through parents and other relationships and experiences in the child's life.
- The first determinant of any current behavior is likely to be found in the parent-child relationship, especially, as we have emphasized, in the pleasure/pain economy of that relationship.
- Behavior evolves through phases in which current levels of psychological and biological functioning influence and are influenced by previous phases.
- Transformation is the main characteristic of this epigenetic evolution.
- No one phase has more importance than any other, and developmental transformations continue throughout the life span.

- Each phase brings something unique to the mix, which may compensate for earlier difficulties or raise prior dormant issues to problematic intensity (Nachträglichkeit, or "deferred action"). (J. Novick and K. Novick 2001)

These assumptions inform our model of parent work in general, as parents constitute a major, primary environmental influence in ongoing ways throughout the child's life. In the specific context of our current discussion of late adolescence, we note the continuing plasticity of the adolescent brain, the opportunity for adaptive identifications, and the particular transformation tasks of late adolescence, with the challenge to young people and their parents to opt for progressive, open-system solutions and set aside old patterns of omnipotent, closed-system functioning.

The role of fathers

When we contemplate the developmental tasks of late adolescence, there is a convergence among transformation of relationships to self and others, realignment of the relationship between the pleasure and reality principles, and the consolidation of identity. We have noticed that many who now accept the importance of parent work in general nevertheless work predominantly with mothers. Various theoretical approaches have also tended to give more weight to the maternal than paternal relationship, but that can lead to rationalized explanations for tolerating father avoidance. Often, practical difficulties in father participation are cited, and those have to be given due weight, but we think there may be other, less-conscious factors involving (K. Novick and J. Novick, 2005, 2013) fears and fantasies of paternal power and retaliation. Both male and female therapists may be subject to such worries.

As we were writing this chapter and thinking about the case described above, as well as many others, we realized that progress in each family depended eventually on the participation of the fathers, especially in our work with late adolescent patients (K. Novick and J. Novick 2013). Whether or not they were initially involved, sooner or later, their active involvement created turning points in the work with each patient. This preliminary finding has technical implications, in addition to the affirmation of the importance of the developmental dimensions referred to above. The role of fathers as a bridge to reality and the outside world is well established (Pruett 1992). In our experience, transformation of the relationship to both mothers and fathers is critical for open-system identity formation in young men and young women alike.

Technically, this impacts the structure of the treatment and the network of therapeutic alliances. When fathers don't engage right away, it is useful for therapists to stay flexible about their participation. Probably even more important is to keep an open mind and hold the father present in our mental map of the patient and family's representational landscape. Then we will be ready to enlist fathers whenever they feel able to join the work.

The importance of the therapeutic alliance

Accomplishment of therapeutic alliance tasks promotes attunement in relationships. Current neuroscience supports the importance of attachment and communication in maintaining brain plasticity and growth (Schore 2000; 2002). It seems to us that there is again convergence between important factors in this late-adolescent work. The therapeutic alliance with parents has been empirically shown to have a significant correlation with treatment outcome (Kazdin, Whitley, and Marciano 2006; Garcia and Weisz 2002; McCleod and Weisz 2005; Novick, Benson, and Rembar 1981). Since the therapeutic alliance tasks correspond with open-system functioning, and one way we conceptualize treatment is in terms of movement from predominantly closed-system to greater open-system self-regulation, it follows then that concurrent parent work, whatever the age of the patient, will contribute to greater therapeutic success (K. Novick and J. Novick 1998; J. Novick and K. Novick 2000; 2002).

In our 2005 book, we describe various sources of resistance to substantive work with parents, discussing social-historical, theoretical, dynamic, and political factors. Here we would add another historical aspect, which stems from the fact that many early child analyses were conducted within a very small group of colleagues. For instance, Melanie Klein analyzed her own children; Anna Freud analyzed several of the children of her best friend and colleague, plus others of their classmates. Under such circumstances, no parent work was possible; no therapeutic alliance with parents could be formed, and no dynamic changes in parents could be initiated and worked through systematically.

The field of child-and-adolescent analysis has moved on, and we think it is now ready to accept the utility and impact of concurrent parent work for all ages, including adolescents. It is still an evolving model with many questions of technique to solve. But our experience of the past twenty years of experimentation allows us to share the following technical recommendations.

Technical recommendations

Make use of the full repertoire of psychoanalytic interventions.

Developmental interference in parenting can be understood as pathology amenable to therapeutic work. It follows then that we consider it necessary and appropriate to use the full conceptual and technical repertoire from individual work with children and adults in the context of parent work. We do not define parent work negatively, that is, in terms of what it is not, or what the restrictions may be. Rather, we see it as substantive, significant, and legitimate in its own right. Parent work, therefore, includes interventions traditionally labeled as "therapeutic," for example, analysis of defenses, verbalization, insight, reconstruction, interpretation, and the use of transference and countertransference for understanding and technique.

In addition to the traditional use of education, support, validation, modeling, facilitating, and so forth that have been staples of parent guidance, we can illustrate the relevance and utility of using the full range of techniques both by the difficulties that arise when the therapist pulls back from using these skills and, in the positive sense, when interpretation and working through are crucial to the success of both of the dual goals of treatment. In our experience, use of the full range of therapeutic techniques in parent work does not compete or interfere with individual therapy for parents. Thus, we may use the full range of our skills without inhibition in the very limited and focused area of parenting.

Successful parent work demands internal conviction and explicit presentation of the dual goals of treatment.

Anna Freud defined the goal of child analysis as restoration of the child to the path of progressive development (1970). We have extended this idea to include a second goal: helping parents achieve the developmental phase of parenthood, that is, restoring parents to the path of progressive adult development, in which parenthood is one phase.

Our view of the parent-child relationship provides a framework for evolving a technique of parent work that encompasses both the resistances and the developmental aids to therapy. The aim of child-and-adolescent analysis can be recast as not only the restoration of the child's progressive development but also as the restoration of the parent-child relationship that has been disrupted by pathology to its potential as a lifelong positive resource for both. Thus, we are mindful throughout child or adolescent treatment of these dual goals of the work.

This idea is not only an implicit assumption but also an active and explicit assertion. We tell parents early in the evaluation that we have these two goals for our endeavors together. We work with this idea until it becomes an intrinsic motivation for continued treatment.

Differentiating privacy and secrecy is central.

When we differentiate privacy and secrecy, it helps us define confidentiality more precisely. We talk with parents and adolescents about the intrinsic privacy of thoughts and feelings but state that actions are public. Safety is the paramount clinical requirement, and it will be destructive of the treatment, and perhaps dangerous to the adolescent, if unsafe actions are concealed. Confidentiality should be maintained in support of privacy, but not as a reflexive collusion with secrecy. Our clinical goal is to make secrecy an object of therapeutic exploration and insight, so that adolescents and their parents can begin to take pleasure in fruitful sharing and communication (J. Novick and K. Novick 2009).

With the goal of transforming his relationship with his parents in mind, I had said to Kevin I would share with him things that came up in my conversations with his parents. Ultimately, he and his parents would have freer communication and pleasure in sharing their experiences with each other.

We have written in a number of places about the crucial distinction between privacy and secrecy, which corresponds with the distinction between reality-based open-system functioning and closed-system power relationships, where secrets are a source of dominance (K. Novick and J. Novick 2005; J. Novick and K. Novick 2009; 2011). Nevertheless, the issue of confidentiality is always the main stumbling block in therapists' minds to doing parent work in adolescent treatments. So we have to devise techniques that reassure therapists that they can protect the patient's privacy, help parents tolerate the frustration of not knowing everything, foster greater communication and sharing between parents and adolescent, and redefine separateness and separation from them.

> We talk with parents and adolescents from the beginning about the difference between privacy and secrecy. Privacy is a given of mental life and a right related to mutual respect between separate individuals. Secrecy is motivated withholding that is often hostile and can carry a connotation of knowledge used to feel powerful in relation to excluded others. Differentiating between privacy and secrecy gives the therapist a needed vocabulary to explore family secrets, parents' secrets, the adolescent's secrets. Failure to make the distinction leaves the analyst vulnerable to a "silent countertransference," an internal resistance to engaging with areas of the patient's privacy, which then can have the destructive impact of turning private matters into powerful secrets. (J. Novick and K. Novick 2009, p. 148)

Concurrent parent work confirms the centrality and importance of parents and their primary parental love for their child.

We talk with parents from the beginning about establishing a partnership (therapeutic alliance) to support their ongoing important role with their adolescent child. Much of the work addresses the externalization of responsibility for staying engaged in transformations. Externalizations can have many different sources, ranging from characteristic defense styles to fatigue and helplessness in the face of adolescent pathology. We work hard in the initial phases of treatment to place parents in their rightful position in the mental life of the adolescent, and the adolescent in the center of the parents' consolidation in the phase of parenthood.

Conclusions

In our experience, we have noticed that most parents come for consultation at a time when they feel angry and helpless and very often terribly guilty and ashamed that they can no longer find their love for their child. But without that love, no treatment and no change can take place.

Part of the analyst's task is to believe that some love is there, and then focus on helping parents access it, recover it, and enhance it. Unless analysts can sincerely work in this realm, we will be unable to respect and care for the parents; without that regard, the treatment will founder, as parents will feel criticized and rejected.

We have attempted to show that our model of dynamic concurrent parent work, with its emphasis on developing an alliance with parents that is based on mutual respect and trust, work that taps into the potential for primary parental love, is effective not only with children but also with adolescents.

Notes

1 Jack Novick is a Training Analyst of the International Psychoanalytic Association and on the faculties of numerous institutes. Formerly Clinical Associate Professor of Psychology, Departments of Psychiatry at the University of Michigan and Wayne State University, he also chaired the Child Psychoanalysis Training at the Michigan Psychoanalytic Institute. Kerry Kelly Novick is a Training Analyst of the International Psychoanalytic Association. Also on the faculties of numerous institutes, she was formerly Lecturer in Psychoanalysis, University of Michigan Department of Psychiatry, President of the Association for Child Psychoanalysis, and a founder of Allen Creek Preschool.
2 We have chosen to use the first person in describing clinical material, both to convey more vividly the immediacy of the interaction, and to add a further layer of confidentiality.

References

Benedek, T. (1959). Parenthood as a developmental phase: A contribution to the libido theory. *Journal of the American Psychoanalytic Association* 7:389–417.
DeVito, E., J. Novick, and K. K. Novick (1994). Interferenze culturali nell'ascolto degli adolescenti [Cultural interferences with listening to adolescents]. *Adolescenza* 3:10–14.
—— (2000). Cultural interferences with listening to adolescents. *Journal of Infant, Child, and Adolescent Psychotherapy* 1: 77–95.
Erikson, E. (1950). *Childhood and Society*. New York: Norton.
Freud, A. (1970). Problems of termination in child analysis. *In The Writings of Anna Freud* 7:3–21.
Freud, S. (1911). Formulations on the two principles of mental functioning. *Standard Edition* 12:213–226.
—— (1916). Introductory lectures on psycho-analysis. *Standard Edition* 16:346–347.
Furman (1995). Preschoolers: questions and answers: psychianalytic consultations with parents, teachers and caregivers. Madison (CY): International University Press.
Garcia, J., and J. Weisz (2002). When youth mental health care stops: Therapeutic relationship problems and other reasons for ending youth outpatient treatment. *Journal of Consulting and Clinical Psychology* 70:439–443.
Hyman, S. (2009). How adversity gets under the skin. *Nature Neuroscience* 12(3):241–243.
Kazdin, A. E., M. Whitley, and P. Marciano (2006). Child-therapist and parent-therapist alliance and therapeutic change in the treatment of children referred for oppositional, aggressive, and antisocial behavior. *Journal of Child Psychology and Psychiatry* 47:436–445.

McCleod, B., and J. Weisz (2005). The therapy process observational coding system-alliance scale: Measure characteristics and prediction of outcome in usual clinical practice. *Journal of Consulting and Clinical Psychology* 73:323–333.

National Research Council and Institute of Medicine (2000). *From Neurons to Neighborhoods: The Science of Early Development*. Ed. Jack P. Shonkoff and Deborah A. Phillips. Washington, DC: National Academy Press.

Novick, J., R. Benson, and J. Rembar (1981). Patterns of termination in an outpatient clinic for children and adolescents. *Journal of the American Academy of Child Psychiatry* 20:834–844.

Novick, J., and K. K. Novick (2000). Love in the therapeutic alliance. *Journal of the American Psychoanalytic Association* 48:189–218.

—— (2001). Parent work in analysis: Children, adolescents and adults. Part 1: The evaluation phase. *Journal of Infant, Child, and Adolescent Psychotherapy* 1:55–77.

—— (2002). Two systems of self-regulation. Psychoanalytic approaches to the treatment of children and adolescents. *Special issue, Journal of Psychoanalytic Social Work* 8:95–122.

—— (2007 [1996]). *Fearful Symmetry: The Development and Treatment of Sadomasochism*. New Jersey: Aronson/Rowman & Littlefield.

—— (2009). Expanding the domain: Privacy, secrecy, and confidentiality. *Annual of Psychoanalysis* 36–37: 145–160.

—— (2011). *Mastery or trauma: The adolescent choice*. Presented at the Conference of the International Society for Adolescent Psychiatry and Psychology, Berlin, September.

—— (2012). Discussion of Victoria Todd's Paper "Saving the treatment: affect intolerance in a boy, his parents, the mental health community, and his analyst. *Psychoanalytic Study of the Child* 66:28–32.

—— (2016). *Freedom To Choose: Two Systems of Self-Regulation*. New York: IPBooks.

Novick, K. K. and J. Novick (1998). An application of the concept of the therapeutic alliance to sadomasochistic pathology. *Journal of the American Psychoanalytic Association* 46:813–846.

—— (2005). *Working with Parents Makes Therapy Work*. Lanham, MD: Jason Aronson/Rowman & Littlefield.

—— (2008). The dynamic interaction of transformations of parental and adolescent defenses: The importance of parent work concurrent with adolescent analysis. Workshop presented at the Annual Meeting of the Association for Child Psychoanalysis, St. Louis, May.

—— (2011). Building emotional muscle in children and parents. *Psychoanalytic Study of the Child* 65:131–151.

—— (2013). Concurrent Work with Parents of Adolescent Patients. *Psychoanal. St. Child*, 67:103–136.

Pruett, K. (1992). Latency development in children of primary nurturing fathers--Eight-year follow-up. *Psychoanalytic Study of the Child* 47:85–101.

Schore, A. N. (2000). Attachment, the right brain, and empathic processes within the therapeutic alliance. *Psychologist Psychoanalyst* 20:8–11.

Winnicott, D. W. (1965). The theory of the parent-infant relationship. In *The Maturational Processes and the Facilitating Environment*, pp. 37–55. New York: International Universities Press.

Young-Bruehl, E. (2011). *Childism: Confronting Prejudice Against Children*. New Haven, CT: Yale University Press.

Chapter 7

Reflections on eating disorders in children and adolescents[1]

Gianna Williams and Roberta Mondadori

Introduction

Anorexia and bulimia are complex syndromes and encompass a broad spectrum of pathologies.

The eating disorder can become a way of life, constant thinking about food, calories, dieting, exclusion of certain foods, exercising, and can become the focal point of life for anorexic and bulimic patients. In less severe cases, one lives a more or less normal life, but the mind is constantly preoccupied with food and the fear of being fat.

Although, in many cases, patients suffering from eating disorders succeed in their studies and show good logical ability in speaking or writing, known as 'emotional logic', the ability to make meaningful connections regarding emotions is often lacking. Thinking seems to be replaced by catchphrases, such as Pedro's sentence, which we will see later, 'Thinking is rubbish'. Logic is also absent in the perception and description of one's own body image.

On the basis of M. Klein's psychoanalytic perspective of object relations, we will emphasise certain themes that, in our opinion are common and central in the development of eating disorders. The conflicts underlying such symptoms very often have to do with the difficulty of accepting dependence on the other.

The first topic we will discuss is the importance of the first relationship between child and mother.

Bion (1962), elaborating on the concepts of projection and introjection, developed the 'container/containment' model, in which the 'maternal reverie' function is described as understanding and processing the child's anxieties. The repeated failure of this function over a long period of time greatly increases the child's anxiety. When the child's messages are not recognised, a fear of the other can develop in the child and, gradually, a fallacious perception of self-sufficiency and rejection of dependence on the other.

In some situations, the process described by Bion of a 'container/contained' relationship is reversed and the child, instead of being contained, becomes the receptacle for maternal projections, perceived as foreign bodies (Williams, 1997).

DOI: 10.4324/9781003351184-8

Sometimes infants and very young children have more or less severe eating disorders that obviously cause concern and anxiety. At this age, difficulties with food can be an index of emotional disturbances in the relationship with parents and, in particular, with the mother, as we will illustrate later with the case of Faruk.

It is worth mentioning that the discipline of infant observation developed by Esther Bick (1964) has increased understanding of the emotional states of very young children. If there is a complete or partial lack of understanding that helps the child digest their emotions, this may interfere with their relationship with food.

The second topic we will address, linked to the previous one, is the role of the father in the mother/child dyad. The existence of the oedipal triangulation is treated from a psychoanalytic perspective by various authors, who describe its fundamental function in creating a space between mother and child. It is a function and not necessarily a person. The concept of dyad is actually a triad concept, as the paternal function, the father in the mother's mind, is a third element: mother-space-child. Britton, in his article 'The missing link' (1989), emphasised the importance of triangularity in development and how difficult it is for some children to find themselves in the lonely corner of the triangle. In order to defend themselves against the pain of exclusion, some children develop unrealistic fantasies, such as that the sexual relationship between parents coincides closely with the number of children.

The attack on the link (Bion, 1958) in the relationship between parents sometimes also breaks mental links and can result in thinking and learning disorders, as we shall see later in Giorgio's case. The paternal function of establishing limits and boundaries is often attacked and the father himself, as we shall see in the cases of Rebecca and Lidia, is denigrated and marginalised.

Very often eating disorders in children disappear, but they may reappear as anorexia pathologies in puberty and adolescence, under the pressure of complex physiological, physical, emotional, sexual and social changes. This is also the time to gradually cope with separation from the family, even if only psychologically.

Some young people in search of a new identity may resort to dangerous manoeuvres in the area of eating. The refusal of food can become an expression of a reaction against parents, family, society and their values.

In working with patients with eating disorders, one sometimes encounters figures from their inner world who are extremely strict and judgmental, and who do not correspond to the reality of their parents. These figures interfere with hope and confidence in the possibility of reparation. The 'voice' of these figures, sometimes even concretely heard, pushes patients down a dangerous slope, as we will see later in Maura's case. Sometimes these harsh, judging voices are projected by the patient in the transference relationship into the therapist. In order for these internal figures to be gradually modified, it is important that the patient introjects the experience of a benevolent figure capable of accepting even the destructive aspects of the patient without judging.

Our third theme concerns the structuring of a narcissistic disorder.

Narcissistic disorder consists of a rejection of the dependence of the other and a turning for support to parts of the self that can also be destructive (Meltzer, 1968, 1973; Joseph, 1982; Steiner, 1993). Our particular psychoanalytic frame of reference is based on M. Klein's object-relations theory mentioned above. One of these destructive parts of the self was defined by Bion as the 'destructive superego' (1962), which has much in common with the internal 'voices' we mentioned earlier. All these destructive parts, also described as a *gang* (Rosenfeld, 1971), offer a fallacious protection from psychic pain and dependence from other external sources of help, by attempting to deny the presence of their own needy part, like the anorexic who denies hunger. The advantage of 'internal gangs' is that they are always accessible, whereas the presence of the other is not.

Before discussing individual cases, we would like to emphasise how, especially in adolescence, attachment to the eating disorder, in this case anorexia, can be tenacious. The presence of a narcissistic structure is also evident in the anorexic patient's rejection of any external help; seen as completely useless and even harmful.

This is the letter that a 16 year old girl wrote to 'her dearest friend':

Dear anorexia,

I love you! I love you because you taught me how to lose weight, how to get closer to what I want. I am happy that you are with me. I knew this would happen sooner rather than later. You were always inside me, but your voice did not make itself felt. Now you speak to me and I obey you.

I know you can help me and that when I listen to you we understand each other. Everyone, everyone except me hates you. I don't want you to leave me or be left by me. I need you. You made me understand my body, understand how to change it. I want ... I WANT to lose weight and you are the only one who wants to help me.

I love you, anorexia; you are a part of me, you are like a growth within me. I have allowed you to grow inside my head and together we have taken control. Stay with me anorexia. I just want us to be left alone. I don't want any more help. I want them to leave us alone! We're happy and we're good together. I just want to be left alone with you, Anorexia. Anorexia and me.

This is certainly a chilling message, showing not only the attachment to the eating disorder and the rejection of any external help, but also the idealisation of an internal ally who will always be there, in a destructive fusion that allows no escape. As mentioned earlier, these are also characteristic features of other narcissistic structures, however, what is unique in patients with such severe eating disorders is the degree of destructiveness and the attraction to death. They are patients who, against their own will, require all available help.

*

In this article we have chosen to illustrate a wide range of clinical examples related to the eating disorder, some about more at risk patients, some less, and ranging in age from early childhood to adolescence.

The cases we will now discuss are very different, but they share some common characteristics, albeit in a less serious way.

Faruk, the child who took milk with his eyes closed

Faruk is a child described in the research of a Brazilian clinician who has worked in hospitals with very young children, some with severe eating disorders.

Faruk's case confronts us with the difficulties of an almost one year old child in receiving food and milk from his mother. Faruk was born into a Somali family at a time of famine in Somalia. The child's mother and father were both very anxious because of the lack of news from their loved ones who moved from one area of Somalia to another in search of food. One of the mother's parents had died at that time and the fate of the others was in doubt; a very painful aspect of situations where a loss is not certain and it is therefore not even possible to begin to grieve.

Faruk's mother was understandably very depressed, not only because of the lack of news from her loved ones, but also because the difficulty of dealing with a very traumatic situation together had led to great tensions in the parental couple. Faruk could not take food from his mother when his eyes were open. He could be fed only when he was asleep and his mother would put the bottle in his mouth.

One might imagine that when the child's eyes were closed, no tears rained down on him, metaphorically, from his mother's very depressed eyes. So if Faruk kept his eyes closed and did not see his mother's face, the food was not coloured by the mother's depression.

This example can be significant in the understanding of symptoms that might appear even later, when a traumatic experience such as that of Faruk's parents would take place during the child's life.

Many anorexic adolescents seem to have developed what has been called a 'no-entry defence' (Williams, 1997). This defence, which may initially be seen as positive as an attempt to protect oneself from something emotionally toxic, can however degenerate to the point of causing anorexic symptoms. The toxicity from which children or adolescents with a 'no-entry defence' defend themselves may also come from transgenerational experiences. It is, in any instance, very difficult to generalise.

However, not all children whose parents have a difficult relationship develop eating disorders. The following example should certainly not be taken as a general rule.

Stefania with dangerous teeth

A more serious example of feeding difficulties in childhood is that of Stefania, who at the age of three and a half is brought to therapy by her parents for her refusal of food. Stefania had been subjected to a long series of medical examinations for two years, from the age of eighteen months, which had not yielded any results. The child had also been hospitalised.

The only foods accepted by her were milk in a bottle or liquidised food. An exception to this was pasta, but only served plain.

The eating problems started at weaning. Stefania was described as an obedient child who had endured very intrusive medical examinations without complaint.

The meetings with the parents had allowed the therapist to formulate some hypotheses about the onset of Stefania's pathology. In the family history, there had been some unmourned losses: a year before Stefania's birth, her mother had lost a child in the third month of pregnancy. Stefania's delivery was very complicated and painful, and the mother was not able to hold the baby for a long time. In addition, when Stefania was two years old, her grandfather had died, who had been very present until then and to whom the child was very attached, but his death had not been explained to her; perhaps in order to protect her from emotions that were considered too strong.

In fact, one might think that it was the parents themselves who were not able to deal with their own anxieties. Somehow, Stefania had found in the rejection of the food, that she perhaps perceived as toxic, a means of escaping from her parents' anxieties. We can think of both a dangerous but understandable defence and a fear of her own aggression towards her parents, manifested by her refusal of solid food, perhaps because she feared that her teeth were a dangerous weapon. Stefania's aggression, however, manifested itself in the tight control she exercised over both her parents, from whom she never wanted to be separated, day and night, and the therapist, who was supposed to do everything she was ordered to do, and sit where she wanted, never in her own chair.

A game that Stefania wants to play during a session is very significant: the girl asks the therapist, whom she calls Ciccia Bomba (Fatty Bomb), to make two balls with plasticine, one, the larger one, called 'the pizza', the other, smaller, 'the poo'. She then crushes and bites them both, observing the imprints left by her teeth.

The name which Stefania calls the therapist is not only derogatory, but becomes more alarming if we think of a nursery rhyme, probably known to Stefania:

'Ciccia Bomba cannoniere, con tre bombe nel sedere, una bomba cade giù, Ciccia Bomba non c'è più.'[2]

We see here the child's great aggressiveness, a real explosion of rage. There is a huge confusion between good food, the pizza, and bad and explosive food, the poo.

Once the confusion is explored in therapy sessions, Stefania can start feeding, and is able to differentiate what is good and nutritious from what is harmful.

Giorgio and the bizarre couple

Among children with excessive selectivity in the choice of food, we will mention Giorgio, who could only eat pasta, bread and cheese, but only if eaten separately. This restrictive diet had begun after weaning, followed by a period of eating only puréed food. Giorgio had great difficulty separating from his parents and, like Stefania, had long refused to use his teeth for chewing.

Giorgio was brought to therapy at the age of eight by his parents, who had realised that their son's feeding difficulties were part of a bigger picture. At the same time, the parents were being seen by another therapist.

Unlike the previous examples, in this case, it is difficult to make a hypothesis about possible links between the child's problems and family history.

The rigidity of the food Giorgio could eat contrasted with the great confusion between what was good and what was bad: Giorgio spoke admiringly of a teacher whom he nicknamed 'Bad Eyes' who did not notice anything, while denigrating another, called 'Good Eyes', who saw everything that was going on. It was clear that the child expected no help from adults, whom he often called 'stupid'. And certainly, stupid was the frog in the pond in his garden, which according to Giorgio, was trying to mate with a goldfish. It is hard to find a more bizarre mating fantasy, a mismatched union between two totally different species. This fantasy seems to show how reluctant Giorgio was to the idea of a creative link between his parents (Britton, 1989, 1998). Mating could only be grotesque and despised, and the fantasy of the frog and the goldfish indicates his attempt to avoid the reality of the union between father and mother.

The mother was perceived as the 'pure water', linked to images of distance, such as the stars, while the father was represented in his games as threatening and contaminating. The water was indeed pure, but it was in a place called 'the cauldron of the devil', thus a dangerous place with a fantasy of possible contamination.

Giorgio's games and tales were full of aggression: there was the desire to dissect every kind of animal to see what was inside, there were water bombs that Giorgio said he wanted to throw at his schoolmates, bombs that would only explode once, and were then immediately destroyed. There were also airplanes that caught fire. Like Stefania, Giorgio was terrified of an explosion that would destroy him and the others.

Giorgio himself, significantly, told the therapist that his mother had told him that his teeth had grown all together at the time of weaning, filling up his mouth. It is impossible not to think of the image of a shark, which the child regarded as an animal to be admired and unjustly slandered. The representations of aggression are extreme, perhaps reinforced by the image of 'a mouth full of teeth'. In addition to the eating disorders, Giorgio also presented considerable difficulties at school, perhaps partly attributable to his refusal to understand and learn what was explained to him, similar to his refusal of food. Another component of the learning disorder that was connected to Giorgio's fierce attack on the link between parents, an attack that is often mirrored by the one on logical links. Learning also requires the capacity to create links (Bion, 1958).

The restrictive diet allowed Giorgio both not to chew, and thus not to identify with the admired but too dangerous shark, and to avoid the reality of the couple represented, concretely, by the combination of different foods, such as pasta that could not be eaten together with Parmesan cheese.

As with Stefania, the help of therapy allowed Giorgio to diminish the control of his food regimen, while the explosiveness of his internal conflict came more to light.

In these psychotherapies, external situations are taken into account, but an attempt is also made to change the internal world of these children and young people, which, as mentioned above, is not a mirror image of the external world, but is very much influenced by conscious and unconscious fantasies (Isaacs, 1948).

Rebecca, the running girl

Rebecca was only eleven years old when she was referred to her GP because she had lost a lot of weight and was 'obsessed with running'. She also refused to stay indoors except at night to sleep, and spent her days on long solitary runs or in the garden, even during the winter months in a northern part of England where the temperature is particularly harsh.

Her problems had coincided with the end of a close relationship with her two brothers, older by some years, with whom she shared male games such as football and cricket, competing with them. This ended when the brothers started to exclude her because she was small and female, preferring the company of male peers. The father, who had often participated in the children's sporting activities, had then withdrawn, Rebecca said, finding himself 'fat and lacking in energy'.

Rebecca had felt completely alone when her partnership with her siblings and father had ended: 'her world had collapsed'. Her school results were excellent, yet for her, weight control and running were the only defences against a sense of total loneliness and the fear of not being able to hold herself together, except with a second muscular skin (Bick, 1964). She said that if she won the running competitions, she would draw attention to herself and everyone would ask: 'Who is that girl?' This actually seemed to be Rebecca's question to herself: she seemed to have lost a sense of her own identity since her association with the male world had ended, and she rejected her femininity by attempting to identify herself completely with a vigorous, masculine figure, which was, however, no longer that of her father.

Another reason for despair for Rebecca was the conspicuous scar on her face, the result of a forceps delivery at the end of a long and difficult birth. She perceived the scar as proof of something wrong within herself: she referred to it as a 'mark of Cain' visible to all.

Gradually, it became clear that Rebecca's refusal of food, together with her refusal to accept the changes to her body, were ways to show her rebellion towards her mother. When her mother prepared a snack for her on the way home from school, she refused it. She later went so far as to prepare her own meals and eat them alone in secret.

Rebecca had been breastfed until she was eighteen months old, then her mother weaned her abruptly. It is possible that the disappearance of the breast, although replaced by the bottle and solid food, had caused her fear of being starved to death and thus having to accumulate nourishment on her own.

Rebecca's aggression towards her mother was increased by the presence of the scar on her face, which she blamed on her mother, who had not pushed her out with enough energy, so that the forceps had to be used. Now Rebecca retaliated against her with the rejection of food, femininity and home.

Another very important element in the family history was the death of the maternal grandmother, which occurred shortly after the child's birth as a result of a serious illness diagnosed during the pregnancy. The relationship between the grandmother and Rebecca's mother had never been good and this could have led to a difficult bereavement. Furthermore, the mental state of the mother during the illness and death of her own mother may have had an impact on Rebecca, as in the case of Faruk, Giorgio and Stefania.

Very gradually, through a long therapeutic process, Rebecca realised that the attacks against her body and her development were also targeted against her mother. She abandoned the fantasy that her mother had inflicted a 'mark of Cain' on her. It was not easy for Rebecca to tolerate the guilt of having mistreated her mother so much, both externally and internally.

One proof of this change was when Rebecca agreed for the first time in five years to go on holiday with her family, thus sharing the house and meals with them: the beginning of a very different relationship with her parents.

It seems that Rebecca finally came out of her narcissistic shell, accepting the food offered by the therapist and her parents. This could only happen due to a change in her internal world's figures: the emergence of trust in the help of the therapeutic relationship took the place of the dangerous relationship with the eating disorder.

Lidia, the wiped-out father

We now present the case of Lidia, a 16 year old girl.

Lidia had had difficulties with food since she was a child, but real anorexia started at the age of thirteen. After a short course of psychotherapy, Lidia's weight stabilised and she was no longer considered at risk. Three years later, however, her parents separated and at the same time, Lidia lost weight so quickly that she had to be hospitalised. During the therapeutic work, Lidia denied that the separation could have been a significant factor. On the contrary, she claimed that her parents should have separated earlier, as they had never got along well.

Lidia no longer wanted to see her father, whom she considered the cause of the family's unhappiness. We can assume that, as in Giorgio's case, Lidia's difficulties with food as a child were already the prelude of an uneasiness in her relationship with her parental couple. This unease, however, had not come to light and now manifested itself violently in the severe refusal of food.

During therapy, it became increasingly clear that there was a serious internal conflict. This conflict manifested itself in her contradictory attitude towards her body image. Lidia knew she was not fat, but at the same time she said she was. She once said in a desperate voice: 'But if I say I don't see myself as fat, they will force me to eat!'

In reality, what Lidia rejected was the transformation of her body, which took away the illusion of remaining a child forever. The female body forced her to think about the meaning of entering the area of sexuality: it had to be avoided at all costs.

Lidia was trapped in a world of thought denial, which constituted a defence for her against the approach of too distressing emotions: the rejection of thought, food for the mind, was similar to the rejection of food for the body.

At the same time, fortunately, Lidia accepted the therapy, however, this did not seem to mean an attempt to get to know herself better, but rather a response to her need for a benevolent presence that did not force her to think. In other words, the search for a supportive and caring mother who imposed neither rules nor the presence of a father and parental function on her. The mother/child pair was the only acceptable one for her. Lidia gave a very good example of how difficult it was for her to have a different image, when she cut out the image of her father from all her photographs.

It was not enough for Lidia that her parents had separated. The father lived elsewhere, but Lidia no longer wanted to see him. His image had to be completely erased, as if he had never existed (Britton, 1989, 1998).

It was only much later that Lidia, driven by the desire to break out of the prison in which she had locked herself up, began to accept the food for thought provided by the therapy, and showed a greater interest in learning more about herself and her past. She recounted on one occasion that she had finally tidied up her room, throwing away most of her old things, but not the diaries she had started writing at the age of thirteen, i.e. at the beginning of the anorexic symptoms. She said that it had been very painful to re-read her own history, however, the diaries represented a part of herself that she did not want to delete; she did not want to go back.

This episode shows how Lidia had become more aware that her growth could only take place through self-knowledge, tolerating the anxieties that may arise from this. She had a desire, therefore, not to destroy the evidence, however disturbing, of her problems. This, up to that point, had been a constant mode in her thought process.

Accepting the help of the therapist, no longer perceived merely as a supportive presence, implied a thinking agent fostering development (Bion, 1962). It was very painful for Lidia, in the context of the therapeutic work, coming to terms with her own aggression towards both parents. Gradually, there was more space in her mind and Lidia began to think 'that not everything that is negative comes from outside'.

At the same time, her rejection of food diminished, and Lidia was finally able to have a life in which there was room for friends and studies, a life other than one dominated by an obsession with counting calories and tormenting herself in front of the mirror.

A very significant progress, certainly related to the change in her relationship with the therapist, was her acceptance of the parental couple. Lidia had gradually come to accept that the therapist could have a partner, i.e., someone in her life with whom she could share thoughts (Britton, 1989). This acceptance could be a support and enrichment for her, and not an exclusion.

It is certainly no coincidence that Lidia started a meaningful relationship with a young man at that time, herself becoming part of a couple, an important step towards adult life.

Maura and the internal gangs

We saw in Lidia a closure to both food and thought. This also implied the presence of an internal conflict that could not in any way be confronted. In her case there seemed to be no internal voices trying to counteract it. Another example of the presence of internal censoring voices is that of Maura, an eighteen year old girl.

Two years earlier, Maura's mother had contacted a therapist because she was worried about her daughter, whom she described as very withdrawn and with great mood swings. She feared that a deep malaise was behind it and hoped that Maura could be helped. Maura initially refused therapy, but two years later decided to accept it.

Maura, although not anorexic, had had periods when she refused to eat. On the same occasions, she also lost her voice for several days. In the early days of the sessions, Maura was unable or unwilling to communicate; sometimes she closed herself off in silence, at other times she spoke in such an abstract and vague way that it was very difficult to get an idea of where she was and what she wanted to say. She would say, for example: 'I hope to get rid of certain things', without specifying which ones, or: 'My thoughts are going round in circles', and she herself spoke of 'a lot of words for nothing' and 'a clutching at straws'. Maura's parents had separated after years of arguments, when the child was three years old. After a period spent in a seaside resort with her father and his family, Maura went to live with her mother in a city. She described, albeit not in detail, the two families and the two environments as very different: the mother's one, sensitive and full of interests; the father's one, violent and not very open to new things.

A few months after starting therapy, Maura, after observing that as usual she did not know what to say, added that in fact she often 'censored' what came into her mind. The therapist realised that the censorship came from an internal judging group. In the same session, Maura later described the characteristics of the group, which 'pretended to protect her', promising to safeguard her from psychic pain (Meltzer, 1967; Rosenfeld, 1971), but now she began to realise that this was not true. Maura added that it was as if every thought was locked in a glass jar, and the only way to get it out was if the jar 'fell and broke'. 'In that case,' she said, 'things came out and could be expressed'. Maura then clarified that she had only been able to start therapy because one of the jars had fallen and broken, allowing the trapped thought of contacting the therapist to come out.

She realised that in the impossibility of choosing what to communicate, there were some things that were not up to her. These 'mechanisms', as she called these obstructions, had become much more powerful since Maura had started talking about herself with the therapist.

It is clear that the basic difference now was about communication with the other, which was quite different from communicating with a diary, as Maura had done in the past. The fear that had prevented her so far was that of experiencing too violent emotions.

This censorious internal group was contrasted by another, more open group, that would be easily silenced. It was thanks to the 'open' group that she could attend school and be in therapy.

These two internal groups appeared in the external reality in the form of two peer groups, which Maura had spoken of in the past, one formed by her high school classmates, the other made up of other young people who resided in the same area where her father lived. In one of her communications, Maura had confided to the therapist that the second group was a very closed group and that, having seen her once in the company of the other group, they had removed her from their Facebook friends as punishment for her betrayal.

It is surprising that Maura was able to describe her internal world and the presence of a censorious and punitive internal gang so clearly within a few months of starting therapy. The reference to the two peer groups had been very casual, and Maura had made no connection, but perhaps somewhere in her mind, there had been a link between the external and internal realities.

It is possible that the fantasy of the accidental breaking of one of the jars was a defence against experiencing guilt towards the punitive gang and fear of reprisals. The explosion of the jar was not intended by her, which shows that in a part of her mind, Maura is still a prisoner of the malevolent gang.

In fact, a short time later, Maura told her therapist that she did not want to continue therapy. When the therapist, in what was intended to be their last session, pointed out to Maura that her cruel internal gang was again making her refuse the nourishment provided by therapy, Maura understood and became open to a new alliance with the therapist.

One can think that Maura had accepted the food provided to her perhaps too greedily and had found again the voice in order to communicate the existence of the inner gang. Afterwards, however, the risk of relying on a parental object, a change that for her represented a real explosion (Bion, 1962) had frightened her. Maura had thus temporarily shut herself away, refusing to continue.

The image of the glass jar which, by breaking, opens the way to therapy, implies the insight that explosions are not always harmful, but can instead be liberating.

It is very positive that Maura was able to move from the dominance of the destructive voices to a therapeutic alliance. Sometimes the grip of destructiveness is very strong and, as Rosenfeld (1971) makes clear, can be reinforced when the patients try to distance themselves.

Catherine's dreams

In almost all presented cases, the children and adolescents were followed in psychoanalytic therapy with good results.

It is difficult to describe the therapeutic journey that leads to change and improvement in the patient. However, we will try to clarify this process by talking about the change in the figures of the internal world of a bulimic teenager, Catherine, as manifested in two dreams that occurred relatively close to each other. Therapy had begun some time ago.

In one of the sessions immediately following a holiday of the therapist, the theme of an alliance of the patient with a destructive part of herself, which had already been faced extensively, returned with violence in the dream that Catherine recounted.

In the dream, the patient tries to get to a University Psychology Centre where she would follow seminars, but cannot find her way. Under a canopy, in a dark place, the girl sees a group of criminals who appear to have just escaped from a prison. They look grimly at a group of old peasant women. One of the criminals breaks away from the group and violently grabs one of the women, the tallest of the group. He then drags her towards his gang, shouting: 'I couldn't find a better one, but at least we have a hole!' Catherine continues to search for the Psychology Centre and is a detached spectator of the attack.

In a later session, Catherine reports another dream about a gang. This time, however, the gang is made up of five or six year old children, like street urchins. One of them, with a shaved head, goes to kick her. Catherine tries to stop him, but is unable to grab him by his hair because it is too short. This scene takes place in front of a primary school, attended by the children. Catherine enters the school to look for the headmaster, who would certainly protect her and expel the aggressive boy.

In the cases presented above, we spoke of the difficulty of accepting dependence on parental figures and of turning instead to destructive parts of the self as typical features of patients with eating disorders and narcissistic structures (Meltzer, 1967; Rosenfeld, 1971; Joseph, 1982; Steiner, 1993). The two reported dreams clearly show these aspects.

In the first dream the patient, resentful of the therapist's holiday, observes a violent attack by her destructive parts, represented by the criminal gang, directed at what is probably a parental figure, i.e., the tallest woman in the group of peasant women. This in the dream represents a mother and, in the transference relationship, the therapist. She is an extremely denigrated figure, who is unable to defend herself against the aggressor and is described by him as a substitute for more beautiful and younger women, merely 'a hole', a place to evacuate the bulimic patient's sexual excitement or the bulimic vomiting. Catherine remains a mere spectator of the slaughter of her parental object by a destructive gang.

In the second dream Catherine is instead involved in first person in an attack by the destructive street urchin, who is also part of a gang that is, however, much less dangerous than that of the criminals. These are in fact children of 5 or 6 years of age. Another substantial difference from the first dream, in which no protective figure appears, is the presence, although not yet apparent, of the headmaster who will certainly protect Catherine and expel the destructive boy.

The two dreams show us an excerpt from the therapeutic path one hopes to take with patients with eating disorders and other narcissistic structures. From the rejection of dependency and the denigration of parental figures, we move on to a weakening of the destructive parts and a turning to a protective figure who can still handle the destructiveness. There are no longer hardened criminals but street urchins, children, as Catherine is no longer a detached spectator of the attacks, but is herself, the agent of this dynamic. The very favourable change in Catherine's internal world figures that occurred between the two dreams is certainly the result of the considerable therapeutic work carried out. The therapist, far from being denigrated, is represented as a benevolent figure, both protective and firm. There is, on the part of the dreamer, an acknowledgement of acceptance, perhaps with gratitude to the help received.

A fragment of family therapy

Mrs. Gomez wrote a letter to a GP asking for help for her son. The letter very insistently requested that 'the designated patient' be seen urgently. This urgency can sometimes indicate that the problem has been lodged in that family member and that splitting processes are taking place.

Splitting and projection were confirmed by the acts of this family, as initially it was difficult to have all members in the same room, at the same time, although family therapy had been suggested.

Initially, four exploratory sessions were offered, at which only a few family members attended. Four more meetings were later offered and, during this second phase, the family finally managed to come to the sessions in full.

The 'designated patient', Pedro, was fourteen years old and born in England to Spanish parents who were both professionals.

At the beginning of the first session, only the mother showed up, saying that her husband could not come because of work and that Pedro refused to leave the waiting room. Perhaps, she said, we would understand why, if she gave us some information about Pedro's problem.

The nature of the problem had already been mentioned in the referring letter, but the mother wanted to give more information. In the letter, the mother wrote that her son refused to go to school, did not study anymore and lay on the couch all day watching television, eating large quantities of sweets and chocolate.

The therapists did not think it was right to leave Pedro in the waiting room alone, so they went to look for him. When Pedro arrived in the room, his first communication was that his parents had no pleasure in life and that they only worked, while he wanted to relax, regain energy by resting and eating a lot, because he loved food so much. Pedro then asked if we could give him a snack.

One of the therapists said that he seemed to want concrete food, not food for thought. Pedro replied that he did not like thinking at all and that 'thinking is rubbish'. This slogan was repeated several times during the sessions.

It is important to mention Pedro's posture during the first sessions, because he was almost lying down with his back against the back of the sofa and his legs spread towards the centre of the room. He kept his hands in the pockets of his windbreaker, forming a kind of bulge on his belly that made both therapists think of a pregnancy.

This was not interpreted, but it is very significant that the therapists' fantasies were moving in the area of a topic that was to prove crucial.

This topic was central in the third session, where again only Pedro and his mother came. The father was 'too busy with work'. The mother said she wanted to talk about something she thought was important. When Mrs. Gomez started to speak, Pedro, who obviously knew what his mother was going to say, jumped up as if he wanted to punch her. One of the therapists got up without saying anything and Pedro sat down again, covering his face with his hands. One could say that Pedro had created a situation that called for the intervention of a firm paternal function.

At this point, Mrs Gomez was able to say that a few months earlier she had become pregnant. A week after she and her husband had told Pedro, she had lost the baby.

The miscarriage had taken place at home. The father was not there but Pedro was present and even saw the mother put 'the thing', as she called it, meaning the foetus, in a bag and saw the blood. The mother had to go to the hospital and Pedro did not want her to go; he was terrified she would disappear and begged her not to go. Pedro remained alone at home. When the mother spoke of this event Pedro said: 'OK, then let's stab each other'.

One of the therapists commented that talking was very different from stabbing people. The pain of injuries certainly does not make one grow, whereas the pain Pedro felt was perhaps necessary to change and evolve. He added that he felt there was a part in Pedro that perhaps wanted to get out of the current state, a part that wanted to grow.

The other therapist said that she agreed with her colleague, but added that it can be very difficult to grow up if you feel that your mother wants another child. Perhaps Pedro could not understand why, when Pedro was there, this was not enough for her. Did he feel guilty as if he was to blame for the loss of the child?

The mother said that at home, Pedro had really become a voracious child, constantly demanding her attention, so much so that it was difficult for her to go to work. The previous Sunday, she had gone out and 'got some air' for a few hours. Pedro had stayed home with his father, 'but his father was always asleep, at least until noon'. At this point Pedro had tears in his eyes. He said that he did not understand why his mother was always angry with him and that he had thought that she would not come home when she left that Sunday.

Later in the session, the mother spoke of how depressed she had been, especially after the loss of her child, and Pedro said: 'It's true, when you enter the room, a cloud of depression enters with you', then he turned to the therapists in an affectionate manner, pretending to be angry, and said: 'And I don't like these two very much either'.

In contrast to this, at the end of the session, Pedro made it clear that he did not want to leave, asking the therapists to repeat some of the things they had said. He wanted them to repeat that 'maybe he had only imagined things'.

It was clear that Pedro was referring to their interpretations of his not wanting to think, as 'thinking is rubbish', and to their assumptions about something he avoided thinking about, but which weighed on him like 'a cloud of depression'.

The therapists did not obey Pedro's request, did not repeat their words, but appreciated that he felt a great relief in no longer thinking of himself as a dangerous person.

From the point of view of Pedro's symptoms, this session was very significant because his craving for sweets and chocolate decreased considerably. During the following sessions, in which his father's obsessive illness finally came to the fore, there were very important changes in the 'designated patient'. For example, during family therapy, Pedro agreed to go back to school.

Pedro was offered individual therapy and his parents also agreed to do couple work with other therapists. Pedro's intensive therapy lasted three years and Pedro stopped saying that 'thinking is rubbish'.

Concluding remarks

We have repeatedly emphasised the importance of psychotherapy for both children (Stefania and Giorgio) and adolescents (Lidia, Maura or even with mother and baby, as in the case of Faruk). In the cases reported, it was a psychoanalytic model therapy, of variable frequency, which is not easy to describe. The work is based on the therapist-patient relationship, favouring fantasies, dreams, associations and above all the careful and punctual examination of the transference relationship.

Other therapeutic models may sometimes be useful; however, we believe that the fantasies of patients with eating disorders are so hidden in the unconscious that a psychoanalytic approach is perhaps the most valid tool.

Many times, however, as in Pedro's case, an initial analytic family therapy (Box *et al.*, 1981) that succeeds in bringing out the problems of the other members of the family unit is very helpful, because it helps the 'designated patient' to identify more clearly the problems of his or her inner world. It also paves the way for individual therapy with one or more members of the family, as in this case.

Another popular approach is to provide a space for the parents and an individual and a separate space with another therapist for the patient with eating disorders. A common opinion of all professionals of different approaches working in this field is, however, the importance of an early intervention so that the disorder does not become chronic and thus much more difficult to treat.

Bibliography

Bick, E. (1964). 'Notes on Infant Observation in Psycho-Analytic Training', in *International Journal of Psycho-Analysis*, XLV, 558–566.

Bion, W.R. (1958). 'Attacks on linking', in *International Journal of Psycho-Analysis*, 40: 308–315. Also in: *Second Thoughts: Selected Papers on Psycho-Analysis* (pp. 106–107). London: Heinemann, 1967.

Bion, W.R. (1962). *Learning from Experience*. London: Heinemann. Reprinted London: Karnac, 1984.

Box, S. (1981). 'Introduction: Space for thinking in families', in: S. Box, B. Copley, J. Magagna, & E. Moustaki (Eds.), *Psychotherapy with Families: An Analytic Approach* (pp.1–8). London: Routledge.

Britton, R. (1989). 'The missing link: Parental sexuality in the Oedipus complex', in: J. Steiner (Ed.), *The Oedipus Complex Today* (pp. 83–101). London: Karnac.

Britton, R. (1998). *Belief and Imagination: Explorations in Psychoanalysis*. New Library of Psychoanalysis. London & New York: Routledge.

Isaacs, S. (1948). 'The nature and function of phantasy', in *International Journal of Psychoanalysis* 29, 73–97

Joseph, B. (1982). 'Addiction to near-death', in *International Journal of Psychoanalysis*, 1982 (63) 449–56, and in *Melanie Klein Today* Vol I, 311–324.

Meltzer, D. (1967). *The Psycho-Analytical Process*. London: Heinemann.

Meltzer, D. (1968). 'Terror, Persecution and Dread', in E. B. Spillius (Ed.), *Melanie Klein Today* (Vol I, pp. 230–238). London: Routledge.

Meltzer, D. (1973). 'Sexual States of Mind'. *Strathclyde*, Perthshire: Clunie Press.

Rosenfeld, R. (1971). 'A clinical approach to the psychoanalytical theory of the life and death instincts: An investigation into the aggressive aspects of narcissism', in *International Journal of Psycho-Analysis*, 1971(52), 169–178, and *Melanie Klein Today*, Vol I, 239–256.

Steiner, J. (1993). *Psychic Retreats*. London: Routledge.

Williams, G. (1997). *Internal Landscapes and Foreign Bodies: Eating Disorders and other Pathologies*. London: Duckworth.

Notes

1 Gianna Williams and Roberta Mondadori would like to thank the therapists who allowed the publication of their cases, which we will quote in alphabetical order: Keila Barbara Alizzi, Stephen Briggs, Sue Brough, Caterina Canepa Croce, Mariangela Mendes de Almeida Pinheiro.

2 Fatty Bomb gunner, with three bombs in the bottom, one of the bombs falls down, Fatty Bomb is no more.

Chapter 8

Aggressive and antisocial behaviour in adolescence[1]

Donald Campbell

Introduction

Delinquency is such a frequent phenomenon among adolescents that it is often dismissed as part of normal adolescent behaviour without further inquiry into the nature of the delinquency or its function for the adolescent. But how can parents assess the seriousness of delinquent behaviour and the risk of repetition? It is not uncommon for parents to feel guilt and or shame about their adolescent's delinquent behaviour. It is also not unusual for parents to try to avoid uncomfortable feelings about their child's anti-social behaviour by minimizing it, ignoring it, or persecuting their child. This chapter aims to help parents cope with their children when they act in a delinquent way by beginning with the assumption that the adolescent's delinquent behaviour functions as a solution to their mental and emotional conflicts.

However, beyond understanding the nature of the delinquent act itself, it's context and precursors, the act and the adolescent perpetrator should be understood within the context of his or her adolescent development, as well as his or her family, residential setting, and peer environment. Parents can increase their understanding of delinquency by learning to work with their adolescent and any other professional disciplines involved. This chapter aims to provide a model derived from psychoanalytic theory and practice for assessing the risk that delinquent acts pose for the adolescent's development. I would like to illustrate this with an incident that occurred with Max.

Max, Mary Lou and me

When I ran a youth club for teenagers in New York City, one of my regulars was a 16-year-old boy I will call Max, a veteran delinquent who was a failure at school and with his peer group, which is why he played the superior tough guy role around the club teenagers. He entertained and intimidated the younger children with tales of petty crime and vivid accounts of his exploits in gang warfare. Then, via the grapevine, I heard that Max had failed his driver's test, which is considered a rite of passage into adulthood by teenagers in the United States.

DOI: 10.4324/9781003351184-9

Much to my surprise, Max came to the club Saturday night. Halfway through the evening, a terrified girl ran over to me shouting that Max had a gun. I didn't move, although my first thought was to get out of the way, duck behind a pillar, or even better, exit unnoticed through a side door. However, a crowd was already cautiously edging up to me while Max flashed a nickel-plated revolver at May Lou, a sexually provocative girl who had always brushed him off. Mary Lou put on a brave face as she backed into a corner. I was now embarrassed by my first thoughts and aware that these adolescents were expecting me to deal with the situation.

Max then turned and approached me. He was tense and giddy with excitement. His face was flushed as he waved the gun at me and said, "Hey, Campbell, how do you like my piece?" I paused for a moment, obviously groping for what to say, and then told him that he was frightening the kids with his revolver, so why not come into my office and show it to me there? In the heat of the moment, at an intuitive level, I had sensed that Max was also frightened. He wanted to appear in control, while also needing me to contain him without leaving him defenceless and humiliated.

Since delinquent activity is always aggressive and involves a second party, it is, as such, antisocial. Whether the delinquent behaviour is aimed at a person's mind (such as lying or trying to deceive), someone's body (as in causing grievous bodily harm, assault or murder, or in Max's case threatening to do so), or their property (by burglary, arson, theft or shoplifting), it is always unsettling for the victim. Delinquent actions do not necessarily disturb, at least consciously, the perpetrator. It is the disturbance, or what Winnicott (1956) called the 'nuisance value' in the antisocial behaviour, which compels the environment to manage the offender.

It was the impact of Max's delinquent behaviour upon me that motivated me to react to Max, in this instance, in a way that enabled him to give up his threatening behaviour. Williams (1983), following Melanie Klein, draws attention to delinquents who evacuate into others by means of projective identification feelings such as anger, envy, confusion, fear and excitement, which have become intolerable. The delinquent act is the vehicle by which the adolescent projects these unwanted states of mind into others (e.g., victims, parents, authority figures, professionals, bystanders, accomplices, etc.). Delinquent behaviour also supports other defence mechanisms, such as denial, splitting, reversal, passive into active and identification with the aggressor. *It is the reliance upon action to project painful thoughts and feeling outside of him or herself and into the environment that is the fundamental characteristic of the delinquent's psychological defences* (Campbell 1997).

When Max brandished his gun, he succeeded in splitting off his fear of women and his anxiety about being mocked for failing his driving test and projected these feelings into Mary Lou, the other teenagers and me. Everyone in the youth club was frightened. Initially, I felt tense and backed away from Max. Max turned his passive experience of being failed by the driving instructor into an active one by dominating the group with his gun. In this way, he reversed the trauma of his failed test and Mary Lou's previous rejections. He was not able to handle a car, but he could control an entire crowd. He was no longer looked down upon by the boys of his age who had their driver's licences. Mary Lou could not brush him off. Max was not frightened about being able to cope, but I was.

However, this tendency to project internal conflict into the other generates a vicious, self-fulfilling prophecy. As pain builds up inside, the delinquent projects it out and others become disturbed and retaliate in obvious or subtle ways to get back at the delinquent instead of trying to control or understand him. This confirms the delinquent's expectation that others will relate to him as he did to them, that is, in a delinquent way. The anti-social child now feels persecuted, not by something inside that he feels unable to deal with, but by their parents, another person or institution, a tangible something, that he can actively, sado-masochistically engage. I will return to this dynamic later, but first, I want to propose a view of two types of aggression that are expressed in delinquent acts.

Ruthless and sadistic aggression

Psychoanalysts have long postulated a self-preservative instinct that is an instinctual response we all possess to stay on the tightrope, to flight to survive as a physically, mentally and emotionally coherent human being. Anything that threatens our physical or psychological survival constitutes a danger. The danger may come from the external world (the demands and limitations of reality) and/or our internal world (our sexual and aggressive wishes, our guilty conscience, depressive feelings, etc.).

Anxiety is a feeling state that alerts us to a present or future danger. We respond to anxiety with defensive manoeuvres, I will call solutions. The 'best' solution is that which creates and maintains a feeling of safety and well-being. A neurotic or psychotic state, a symptom, a character trait, a defensive mechanism, or a criminal act, however maladaptive in the outside world, may be the 'best' solution that an individual can negotiate given the external circumstances and his/her internal resources (Sandler and Sandler, 1992).

When these solutions or defensive manoeuvres are effective, they are invisible to us and others. In fact, all of us employ a variety of invisible defensive solutions to problems which we encounter every minute of every day. Aggression is just such a solution. However, when aggression is employed as a solution it makes an impact on the victim, the parents and the authorities.

I view all aggression as primarily self-preservative, but it may take two forms: ruthless or sadistic. Ruthless aggression is, I believe, the earliest defensive solution and is manifest as the capacity for fight or flight when we feel that our survival is at risk. However, the exercise of ruthless aggression is not without its liabilities, as is apparent in a conflict faced by that earliest exponent of ruthless aggression – the baby. When a baby's wellbeing is disturbed by hunger, cold, physical pain, frustration, etc., he resorts to physical solutions or what I call *primary defences*, that is a large and diverse repertoire of physical responses which include motor reactions, such as muscular tension, clenched fists, waving arms, violent kicking and screaming, which temporarily alter the infant's physiological state by affecting blood pressure, temperature, etc. When this occurs, the child associates these motor responses with getting rid of painful or frightening feelings. As the infant begins to distinguish between itself and others, it is not unusual for him to perceive his mother as the person who is responsible for the pain he feels. When this occurs, the child directs a physical reaction towards the mother. This is an early expression of ruthless aggression, which aims to get rid of an object that is perceived as threatening the survival of the self.

However, in this situation, intimately linked to the original threat to physical survival (say, hunger due to the mother's failure to feed), the child now becomes aware of a second anxiety aroused by the threat of eliminating the very person upon whom he is dependent for his survival – the mother. The threat of losing the mother due to the child's aggressive attack and/or abandonment by her in retaliation motivates the child to transform its destructive aim of aggression (the getting rid of the mother) into an aim to control her via sadism. The fear of loss of the mother is changed into pleasure derived from making her suffer and witnessing that suffering.

During an act of ruthless violence at any age, the fate of the object is irrelevant once the threat to physical or psychological survival posed by the object has been removed. During a sadistic attack, the aim is not to destroy the object but to preserve it in order to control it. In order to assess the danger posed by an offender, it is important to identify whether the delinquent act is primarily an expression of ruthless or sadistic aggression. A delinquent act that has been mobilised solely by ruthless aggression aims only to negate a threat to physical or psychological survival. The perpetrator has, in carrying out a physical or sexually aggressive act, no relation to the victim other than to eliminate the threat which the victim poses: the feelings and fate of the victim in this context are not relevant. Consequently, a victim of ruthless aggression is at greater risk than someone who is treated sadistically. A sadistic attack aims to control the object, exert power over it, and not eliminate the other.

Adolescence

Usually, during the phase of development which precedes puberty, which we refer to as latency, Oedipal wishes to have a sexual relationship with the parent of the opposite sex and get rid of the parent of the same sex are repressed. However, the physiological and hormonal changes, which take place during puberty, and which initiate the adolescent process, thrust the sexual and physical body into the forefront of the adolescent's mental life. With the emerging appearance of a man or woman, the adolescent can, for the first time, enact what he or she could only wish for previously. After puberty, the adolescent has the capacity to impregnate or bear children and the potential strength to convert into reality any wish to kill the rival parent. This newly developed sexual maturity heightens wishes and anxieties about sexuality and puts pressure on the adolescent's defences aimed at maintaining the incest barrier. In this developmental context, the boy and girl face the fundamental tasks of adolescence: assuming ownership of a sexually potent body that is separate from the parents, in the context of heterosexual relationships with non-incestuous objects.

The pain associated with the awareness of the failure to integrate genital sexuality with heterosexual relationships outside the family motivates many adolescents to search for excitement in delinquency. The physical excitement experienced by the delinquent before, during and after an offence is linked to their emerging sexuality. In my view, an adolescent's delinquent act, whether it is motivated by ruthless or sadistic aims, is the fulfilment of a sexual fantasy and, as such, it generates sexual excitement, which momentarily blocks out internal distress.

When viewed from this perspective, delinquent behaviour can be seen as an enactment of an internal conflict that becomes intolerable and can no longer be dealt with internally. Whatever has precipitated the current emotional crisis for the delinquent, is likely to be linked to traumatic, perhaps now unconscious, events of childhood over which the child had no control. These earlier childhood traumas are revived by puberty and must be dealt with again during adolescence. For this reason, I believe that minor delinquent acts, especially those which occur *within* the family, or are clearly seen as *enactments of current family conflicts* would benefit from therapeutic work with the family. Helen and Roger are two examples of such cases that I saw in the course of my psychotherapeutic work with offenders at the Portman Clinic.[2]

Helen: Stealing as a hopeful response to early deprivation

Helen was referred to the Portman Clinic after her mother discovered she had stolen jewellery from the mother of two children she had been working for as an au pair. Helen had been stealing from her own mother and shops for as long as she could remember.

Helen's father was away on business so much that he felt like a stranger to her. While she was extremely possessive and protective of Helen's older sister, Mother handed over the care of Helen to a succession of nannies, some good and some bad, who were all, in the end, found to be inadequate by Mother and abruptly sacked. Mother also kept the family isolated from the rest of the village behind the walls of the grandest house in the area. Helen put on a cheery face, and denied the deprivation she had experienced. Her 'solution' was to identify with her mother's possessiveness and, in this way, she managed to feel close to her mother without being smothered by her as she felt her older sister had been. Helen's stealing from other mothers, or taking objects associated with her own mother, appeared to serve at least two functions: it was the means by which Helen displaced her enormous rage towards her mother onto mother substitutes who were, like Helen herself, forced to suffer the loss of something valued; it also enabled her to reverse the experience of deprivation and loss which she could not control by actively taking from another mother figure what she could not get from her own mother.

Donald Winnicott (1956) held the view that where an anti-social tendency exists, there has been what he called 'a true deprivation'; that is to say, there has been something good and positive in the child's experience up to a certain date that was then withdrawn. The withdrawal extended over a period of time which was really too long for the child to keep alive a memory of the good experience. Winnicott always believed that lack of hope was the basic feature of the deprived child. However, it is during the anti-social time that the child is actually expressing hope because it believes that the environment is there to be contacted and will respond, albeit in a punitive way.

Helen's stealing represented, at one level, her search for something that was good and had been lost. She was trying to take back a mother upon whom she still believed she had a child-like claim. However, Helen's attempt to master the deprivation of her childhood by stealing also served to defend against properly mourning the loss of the good experience that Winnicott referred to. Helen invited her mother to discover her delinquency by leaving the stolen jewellery on top of her chest of drawers in order to provoke containment and restraint. Helen, like other delinquents, unconsciously wished that her mother (or those authorities who represent Mother) would respond to her stealing by taking care of her. In this way, Helen tried to master the relationship that she originally could not control to her satisfaction.

While Helen illustrates the influence of early deprivation on later delinquent behaviour, Roger is an example of a delinquent 'solution' to later Oedipal conflicts as they are revived during adolescence.

Roger: Exhibitionism as Oedipal triumph, revenge and punishment

Roger, a diffident, passive sixteen year old, had been exposing his genitals to women for six months but had only recently been apprehended by the police for the first time. He said that the excitement and fear associated with risk were the strongest feelings. A smile crept across his face when Roger described the 'surprised' look on the woman's face. Roger did not know why he did it. Exhibiting himself did not, in any way, fit the image he had of himself. But, then, he was not sure who he was anyway. He admitted that he would rather not think about exposing himself and thought he would never do it again, now that he had been caught. When he exposed himself, Roger explained that he was in a state of mental confusion, at war within himself and cut off from everything around him which was outside a three-yard cube. The war inside was described as one part of himself trying to stop another part from exposing himself. He seemed disassociated from both. Only the fear of being caught ever restrained him. However, when his 'defences were down' or when he was 'a little drunk' he felt out of control and unable to stop himself. At no time did Roger convey any concern for the women he exposed himself to.

Roger started 'flashing' shortly after his eighteen year old brother's girlfriend Caroline moved in to live with the family and share a bed with his brother. Roger told me that the occasion that resulted in his being arrested was unlike all the others because he exposed himself from a window in his parents' bedroom (while his mother was away) to women passing by on the pavement.

His father, a high-ranking police officer, had little time for Roger and appeared to have been dominated by his ambitious and unpredictable wife. There were rows and a chronic state of tension between his parents. Mother returned to pursue a high-powered career in advertising when Roger was six months old and left him in the care of au pairs. Roger gave me the impression that he grew up with a narcissistic mother who was withdrawn and preoccupied at times and close and intimate at other times. Roger said that she related to the whole family via 'emotional blackmail'. He would wait for her to come home from work and study her face to see what sort of mood she was in so that he could determine whether she was approachable or not. If he got it wrong or tried to confront her, she would attack him for his insensitivity towards her and then become sullen and withdrawn.

Mother's reaction to Roger telling her about his offence illustrates the intrusive, seductive dimension to their relationship. Mother was lying in bed with the curtains drawn, Roger sat on the bed, told her what he had done, and they 'cuddled'. His mother reported to me that she told Roger that perhaps he had "his father's physiology". His father wakes up every morning with an erection. If Roger had the same physiology, his mother said, it must be difficult for him to cope with his erections. After all, his father had herself right there every morning, but Roger had no one.

Recently, Roger had become more concerned about his inability 'to get beyond friendships with girls'. Roger confirmed my view that his relationship with his mother and the tension between his parents may well have contributed to his difficulties in developing sexual relationships with girls. He agreed that he felt more despair when he compared himself with his brother, who was sleeping with his girlfriend, Caroline, and was particularly upset when she moved in. He felt crowded out of his own house. All this left him feeling depressed and sorry for himself. After all he went through growing up in his family, after all the hassles from stupid and insensitive teachers at school, why should he have to contend with the police and court? All he could think of was, "Why me?"

As early as 1916, Freud (1916) remarked upon children who were naughty on purpose to provoke punishment and were then content after being punished. He believed that these misdeeds were motivated by an unconscious sense of guilt arising from repressed Oedipal wishes to kill father and have sex with mother. Both the guilt and its source were unconscious. The adolescent who is overwhelmed by guilt arising from the revival of Oedipal fantasies may commit delinquent acts in order to attach the guilt to something conscious and find some temporary relief when he is caught.

Freud's theory is useful in understanding why Roger moved into his parents' bedroom in order to exhibit himself after months of exposing himself on the streets without being apprehended. It would appear that the incestuous excitement aroused by being sexually active in his parents' bedroom also increased his guilt and anxiety about being able to control himself as he moved closer to his parents. Roger's revenge and triumph over his oedipal rival are evident in his violating the parental bedroom, exposing his father's ineffectual defence of the incest barrier to his police colleagues and the court and shaming his law enforcement father who raised a son who committed a crime. The sadistic gratification derived from his encounters with women is also evident in Roger's pleasure in the 'surprise' the woman registers in response to the sudden exposure of his penis. Roger unconsciously behaved in such a way as to ensure that law and order would be brought into the parental bedroom and that his Oedipal guilt would be punished.

Roger also brings to mind Freud's (1916) paper about those characters who feel they are justified in no longer submitting to any disagreeable reality. They feel they are *exceptions* because they have already suffered enough, unjustly so, during their childhoods. I believe Roger sees himself as an exception. The process of taking responsibility for his exhibitionism, acknowledging that he committed an offence and facing up to the reality of that image of himself, and then thinking through, albeit with a professional's help, why he did it, represents a disagreeable reality for which he would like to claim an exemption because he has already suffered enough.

Differential diagnosis

No two victims or offenders are identical, and a differential diagnosis is required if we are to understand the individual adolescent. A differential diagnosis should include (1) the study of the offence itself, (2) a psychosexual developmental history of the child or adolescent, including, (3) family history (for sources of identifications and signs of collusions as well as the onset of delinquent or pre-delinquent behaviour), gender influences, racial and cultural backgrounds, and (4) the nature of his or her childhood and adolescence. The aim is to develop a picture of the internal world of the adolescent victim or offender. It is likely that an in-depth study of a perpetrator will discover an early history of victimisation.

Details of frequency and persistence of delinquent behaviour over time contain important clues to understanding the nature and function of the offence or the role played by the victim. The setting and the relationship with the victim are also important: was he or she a relative, a friend or a stranger? How old was the victim? The victim's account and details of the act may also give us clues about the severity of the offence and the adolescent's disturbance.

I want to illustrate the value of a differential diagnosis by considering a specific group of offenders, namely adolescent child sexual abusers. In light of the fact that approximately half of the adult sexual offenders coming before the courts began their sexual deviancy in adolescence (Davis, 1987), one can see the enormous prophylactic potential in work with adolescent abusers. Care should be given to any consideration of transferring an adolescent child sexual abuser to a criminal court since there is a need to consider their offences in a family context in order to identify patterns of collusion with the adolescent's individual psychopathology.

Adolescence is such a turbulent and complex phase of development that it is difficult to categorise adolescent abusers by their behaviour, but it is helpful to try to locate them along a continuum from less to more severe disturbance.

At the less severe end of the continuum are the adolescent abusers whose sexual identity is heterosexual. In their masturbation fantasies and sexual daydreams, these adolescents are involved with adult or contemporary female partners. Their sexual abuse of children is infrequent, not persistent, and done in reaction to rejection by or anxiety about approaching female peers. There is no overt violence. Although they relate to the child on the basis of their own needs, they recognise that he or she is an independent person and they respond with shame and guilt to their abusive behaviour.

Sidney's first offence

Sixteen-year-old Sidney was babysitting an eight year old girl he had known for several years when he fondled her genitals and climbed on top of her. Two weeks earlier, his first girlfriend had broken up with him to go out with an older bloke. Sidney's mother who worked a day shift, denigrated Sidney's father who worked a night shift. Sidney felt estranged from his father. Sidney felt uncomfortable when his parents tried to minimise the incident and sought help so he could have a proper girlfriend.

This was Sidney's first offence. He represents the kind of offender who could benefit from referral to the family justice system where his case is more likely to be quickly expedited and where he is less likely to be stigmatised as a criminal.

At the more severe end of the continuum is the adolescent whose sexual fantasies are exclusively about children. Their abusive fantasies and behaviour are frequent, persistent, often accompanied by violence, and function to defend against a psychotic breakdown. They show no concern for their victim. In contrast to the less severely disturbed abuser, this adolescent sees the child as existing only to gratify his needs. These adolescents are usually lonely, isolated from their peers and uninterested in adult homosexual or heterosexual relationships.

Harry: A persistent offender

Harry is 17, unhappy, friendless, unemployed and living in a hostel after his third offence of indecent assault on ten-year-old boys. On the last occasion, Harry forced a boy to go on to the roof of a high-rise block of flats. Harry began truanting from school at 12 and spent his days riding buses around London in order to look at young boys and daydream about buggering them. During my interview with Harry for a Court Report, I discovered that he had nurtured a suicide fantasy and had made a suicide plan. Although I alerted the hostel staff to the risk of suicide, Harry's determination was such that he eluded the staff supervision at the bail hostel and tried to hang himself while awaiting trial.

Harry's abusive behaviour was chronic, severe and clearly outside his home. Not surprisingly, Harry's single-parent mother had abdicated her parenting role when Harry began truanting. Harry's dangerousness merits his being seen within the criminal justice system.

Assessing risk

Discussions regarding the treatment, management and placement of child offenders and their victims should take into account the risk of the offender repeating delinquent behaviour as well as the risk of the victim finding themselves or putting themselves in dangerous situations. If William Kvaraceus (1934) was right when he said 'nothing predicts behaviour like behaviour', a study of an offender's behaviour over the course of his life should give clues about his potential for dangerous behaviour in the future. Three categories in Nigel Walker's (1991) *Typology of Dangerousness* provide a useful framework for considering an offender's behaviour as well as the behaviour of the victim. The first category is the conditionally dangerous individual represented by (a) those who are brought into situations of provocation by inclination. There are two categories among the unconditionally dangerous: (a) the opportunity seeker, i.e., someone who searches for opportunities to be delinquent, and (b) the opportunity maker.

My impression from studying patients at the Portman Clinic is that those whose delinquent behaviour was primarily ruthless tended to be more seriously disturbed and suffering from primitive anxieties with paranoid orientations to others. Those patients who resolved conflicts primarily through sadistic behaviour, either sexual or physical, tend to be less disturbed and more object oriented. Perversions (of which sadism is always a component) function as solutions to neurotic or psychotic anxiety by encapsulating the mental disturbance in the perverse activity. Therefore, one should be cautious about an assessment of the severity of mental illness when dealing with perverse patients. The 'successful' perversion often enables the perpetrator to function more or less normally in society often exercising authority, as we know, in public life, which contributes to genuine shock when offending or perverse behaviour is discovered. Consequently, the offending behaviour appears 'out of the blue', and is considered irrational or without psychological explanation.

Roger and Harry were unconditionally dangerous. They were opportunity seekers. There was a driven quality about their offending. Helen was a borderline case. She was inclined to steal from mothers, but she did not look for victims. However, she took advantage of opportunities to steal when she was babysitting, just as she had done from her mother. Sidney, on the other hand, was conditionally dangerous. He did not search for girls to molest, but was not able to resist the temptation to abuse the girl he was babysitting.

The impact of child abuse on development

An act of child abuse bisects the line of normal development and disrupts the natural timing of the biological clock, turns the Oedipus complex upside down, and undermines the 'bedrock of reality' by challenging the view that children are not the same as adults and males and females are different. Incestuous wishes are gratified with parents, siblings, or adolescents or adults who are perceived as siblings or parental substitutes. The sexually abusive act over-stimulates the mouth, anus, or genitals. These traumatised erotogenic zones must be incorporated into the child's sexual body image.

Likewise, the experience of being overwhelmed by a genitally mature person will reinforce passive submissiveness and undermine the normal progress toward heterosexual relations in adolescence. For instance, a boy who is buggered may feel he has been feminised, used like a woman and find it difficult as an adolescent to think of using his penis in relation to a woman. As a consequence, the abused child can be expected to think of himself or experience himself in pre-genital and pre-oedipal terms.

Whatever the relationship between a child and his abuser, the child will directly or indirectly feel that the parents are responsible, if only for failing to protect his body. Behind the child's feeling that the parents have failed to play the role that is needed and expected of the adult generation is a sense that if the parents had been turned into what he or she felt about his or her body they would have protected their child. The parents who fail to respond appropriately to their child's abuse confirm the child's feeling of abandonment. When the abuse is unshareable, it is unacceptable, and the rage, fear and sexual excitement cannot be psychologically digested. Most children need the help of a parent, close friend, relative, or professional to help them work through the helplessness, betrayal of trust, anger and sexual confusion generated by their abuse. If left alone, the child is likely to repress, deny or disavow the traumatic experience; shame, guilt (conscious and unconscious) and fear of retaliation haunt the victim. All this is rekindled and intensified when the child victim enters puberty.

The adolescent, who was abused as a child, is likely to be confused about his sexual identity, feel guilty about and ashamed of his pre-genital fantasies and be ill-equipped for the tasks of adolescence. He may feel a failure and be unable to identify with his peers. When separation from his parents becomes too frightening and the prospect of genital contact with peers is too dangerous, the abused adolescent looks for a sexual partner among children.

Working with parents of delinquent adolescents

The decision about how to work with the parents and/or family of a delinquent adolescent will need to be decided on a case-by-case basis. However, in each case the adolescent's developmental state regarding his or her sexuality and the relationship with his parents, as his Oedipal objects, should be given priority. I have not known about a delinquent act that was not also, in some way, a solution to a sexual conflict and, therefore, sexually gratifying.

Mervin Glasser (1977) has outlined three phases of adolescence, which are useful to keep in mind when thinking about whether or not to include the parents and/ or siblings in work with the adolescent, or to work with them separately.

The first phase from puberty to about 14 or 15, which Glasser refers to as early adolescence, is characterised by narcissistic self-involvement and relationships that are oriented around satisfaction of the adolescent's own needs. Delinquent activity during this phase is often characterized by a striking lack of awareness of the other's needs or anxieties when the adolescent feels and acts like a demanding toddler.

Glasser believes that the middle stage of adolescence (roughly between 15 to 18) may be influenced by the adolescent's readiness to challenge parental authority (and its cultural representatives) as he or she strives to become separate and independent. This developmental move away from the parents may take the form of rejecting their values, codes of behaviour and political beliefs, sometimes expressed in delinquent acts. This may lead to joining gangs as the adolescent moves toward deeper (sometimes transitory) involvement with peers. The middle phase is often the most turbulent time for the adolescent as the shifts between dependency and assertions of independence can be swift, extreme and bewildering for the parents and the adolescent alike.

The boundaries between each of the first two phases of adolescence are porous and variable. The late stage, roughly between 18 and 21 or even into the mid-20's, is usually a time of consolidation of the adolescent's sexual identity. While the beginning of adolescence is easier to identify because of the physiological and psychological changes initiated by the onset of puberty, the end of adolescence, without the earlier physical 'markers' of puberty, is more elusive.

Although I have emphasized the role of sexuality throughout development in the conversion of ruthless aggression into sadism, it is during adolescence that the Oedipal conflicts are revived and will provide the unconscious motivation for delinquent behavior. Roger (page) is a case in point. As Melanie Klein wrote in 1927: "It is just anxiety and the feelings of guilt which drive the criminal to his delinquencies. In committing these, he also partly tries to escape from his Oedipal situation" (p. 184). As we can see in the case studies that I have presented, delinquent acts gratify unconscious sexual fantasies rooted in the Oedipal dynamic. The adolescent will fiercely defend against these unconscious fantasies becoming conscious by splitting and denial and repression. At other times, the adolescent will accept punishment as a means of expiating guilt, especially if the Oedipal associations remain unconscious. This resistance makes individual work with delinquent adolescents a slow and often unrewarding process. It also makes working with families of delinquents such a 'dangerous' undertaking because the parents are unlikely to have resolved their own Oedipal conflicts with their children. In such a situation, both the children and their parents have a stake in resisting any exploration of unconscious Oedipal dynamics.

As the practitioner makes an assessment of the delinquent's relationship with his or her parents, the professional will also decide whether or not to work with the parents (and other family members) separately or with the adolescent. The systemic and psychoanalytic issues are too complex to explore within the limited scope of this chapter, but the reader will find a more thorough exploration of work with parents in Kerry and Jack Novick's Chapter in this volume *Considering Concurrent Work with Parents of Adolescent Patients.*

The impact of offending behaviour on professionals

We would expect the anxieties and rage projected through the delinquent act by the offender and aroused within the victim to affect those professionals who are collaborating on the case. The delinquent is likely to see it's parents, mental health professionals and those in the legal system as dangerous, as enemies, even as predators trying to take away his delinquent behaviour. Bearing in mind that offending behaviour is a solution to conflict, one would expect that anxieties would be increased in the offender because of his fear of the consequences of the loss of a solution. Consequently, for the offender, the bind is something like this: how to get help without having his aggressive solutions (the capacity to commit offences) taken away leaving him more vulnerable and helpless. Although it may not be apparent to the lay observer or indeed other professionals who have not had an opportunity to treat offenders over a long period of time, my experience is that most offenders have cruelly persecuting consciences, which continually burden them with bad feelings about themselves. These offenders often feel that the therapeutic and legal processes reinforce their self-denigration.

There is a particular defence against a persecuting conscience, which I find in adult and adolescent child sexual abusers, which may mislead those who are attempting to assess risk. I refer to this defence as the *chameleon defence.* In order to escape from severe self-criticism, the perpetrator unconsciously splits off and disavows the abusive part of himself and employs a chameleon-like facility to identify with external representations of one's conscience, such as idealised parents or authorities with statutory responsibilities, or even the judge himself. This is not a self-conscious pretence. The abuser actually believes that he or she is an ideal parent, caring childcare worker, or wise administrator, and is their child victim's best friend, sensitive babysitter, or helpful tutor.

These chameleon identifications are so believable for the professional because the perpetrator is a believer himself. Consequently, the abuser's internal world and motivation for change is difficult to assess, as is any sign of behavioural change. The abuser may all too readily identify with the attitudes and behaviour promoted by the caretakers, including acknowledgement of his own abusive behaviour, in order to believe he is a good client and win external approval. Issues of what is good and what is bad are preferable to facing more painful anxieties associated with fear of mental breakdown or looking again at an original overwhelming trauma, such as their own experience of being abused as children.

Conclusions

I have tried to show how any assessment or treatment approach that adopts an authoritarian role or focuses exclusively on behavioural change without understanding the paedophile's internal conflicts and anxieties is in danger of being sabotaged by the abuser's capacity to adopt language, concepts and whatever is suggested as normative behaviour by the therapist, probation officer, or forensic psychiatrist, in the same way as the chameleon changes it's identity to avoid being 'found out' by a predator. However, if the chameleon defence is not discovered and it's function understood, the delinquent's underlying anxieties will not be relieved, and the abuser will be at risk of returning to abusive behaviour as a solution once the external supports have been taken away and old anxieties re-emerge. Put into the language of child abuse, any assessment, treatment or management programme that does not take the abuser's internal world into account is very likely to be victimised in the same way as the child victims are, that is by being deceived by the outwardly positive but inwardly fraudulent behaviour of these offenders. This is, in fact, a repetition of the act of child abuse that arouses hope and trust in order to destroy both in the soul of the child.

Notes

1 This chapter is a revised version of an earlier paper (Campbell 1989).
2 The Portman Clinic is an outpatient National Health Service Trust facility which offers psychoanalytically oriented assessment, treatment and management to patients of any age and both sexes who are violent, delinquent or suffer from a sexual deviation.

References

Campbell (1997) 'Assessment of risk in the family justice system', in 'Rooted Sorrow', ed. Hon. Mr Justice Wall, Jordan Publishing, Bristol, pp. 94–105.

Davis GE (1987) 'Adolescent sex offenders'. *Psychol Bulletin*, **101**, pp. 417–427.

Freud S (1916) *Some character types met within psychoanalytic work S E 5*. London: Hogarth Press.

Glasser M (1977) 'Homosexuality in adolescence'. *British Journal of Medical Psychology*, **50**, pp. 217–225.

Klein M (1927) 'Criminal tendencies in normal children'. In *Love, guilt and reparation and other works*. London: Hogarth, pp. 170–185.

Kvaraceus W (1934) *The community and the delinquent.* New York: World Book.

Sandler J, Sandler A-M (1992) 'Psychoanalytic technique and theory of psychic change'. *Bulletin Anna Freud Centre*, **4**, pp. 35–51.

Walker N (1991) 'Dangerous mistakes'. *British Journal of Psychiatry*, **158**, pp. 752–757.

Williams (1983) 'Nevrosi e delinquenza: uno studio psicoanalitico dell'omicidio e di altri crimini'. Borla Publisher, Rome.

Winnicott D (1956) 'The anti-social tendency'. In *Collected papers* (1958). London: Tavistock, pp. 306–315.

Chapter 9

Assessing the risk of self-harm and suicide in adoelscence

A psychoanalytical perspective

Robin Anderson

Introduction

Suicide, attempted suicide, and other forms of self-harm are rare in younger children, but once adolescence is reached the rate of deliberate self-harm rises steeply. In 2000, the suicide rates per 100.000 for 10 to 24 year olds in England and Wales for males and females were 8.8 and 2.6 respectively. In 2023, the rates were 7.4 and 3.1. (Office for National Statistics). This is almost certainly an under-estimate, because of the reluctance of Coroner's courts in this country to bring a verdict of suicide for all but the most certain cases. Even so, mortality rates were higher only for accidents. (Of course, many fatal teenage accidents may have a suicidal aspect to them as well.)

The rate between 2000 and 2023 is relatively stable, and although the figures are smaller for adolescents than adults, it can be seen that males are much more likely to actually end their lives by suicide than females are. Each of these figures represents a major tragedy for a family and for the community they live in and indeed are themselves risk factors for further self-harm and even suicide.

The effect on others of an adolescent suicide cannot be overestimated. It is a trauma that is devastating for other family members, who frequently suffer for years afterwards. Siblings can have their own development grossly interfered with, and are at risk of suicide themselves. It is also deeply upsetting for the surrounding community, especially in schools and university campuses, where it can trigger off waves of suicide attempts or even actual suicides. When the young person has been receiving help from professionals it is very upsetting for them too, giving rise to strong feelings of guilt and distress and loss of a sense of competence, often not helped by the ensuing inquiries which can become dominated by hostile and blaming attitudes which are at the heart of suicidal behaviour and the response it can evoke.

It has been argued that those who attempt suicide are a different population from those who actually kill themselves, but this seems unlikely. A study in Oxford by Hawton et al. (1997) showed that there was a parallel increase in the rate of attempted suicide during a similar period. Empirical studies in the psychiatric literature in relation to the risk of suicide conclude that young people who are

DOI: 10.4324/9781003351184-10

depressed are far more at risk of suicide than those who are not, and that those who attempt suicide immediately identify themselves as part of a group at particular risk. Studies vary, but if the risk of suicide in the general population of adolescent boys is 0.006 per cent, the figure for those who have attempted suicide is 1 per cent in the twelve months following the act. In other words, the chances increase by a thousand times (Hawton & Fagg 1988).

Other risk factors which appear to be important are: a history of being bullied, of being sexually abused, and, for young men, of being imprisoned. Suicidal thoughts and wishes are also common in adolescents. Sometimes they are transient, and not signs of serious risk. Those with persistent ruminations about suicide are likely to be depressed and are at risk of suicide.

As I will attempt to show in this paper, an assessment of risk consists in paying attention to known risk factors, and then putting these into an overall context of the young person's situation at the time of the assessment, their history, and their personality characteristics. Insofar as circumstances permit, the more information that is available the greater chance there is of finding an explanation of the young person's behaviour. Often, we get only a partial picture of what is going on, either in the mind of the patient or in their external life history; but the more coherent and convincing the explanation based on an appraisal of internal and external facts, the more we are able to take appropriate action. It is also true that a sound understanding of the patient's state of mind has a calming effect, both on the patient and on those carrying the anxiety and responsibility. In other words, a good assessment can reduce the risk.

Putting the risk into context

The adolescent process

The reason why adolescents are more at risk than younger children becomes somewhat clearer with a consideration of the biological, psychological, and social changes of adolescence. Adolescents are thrust into a state of rapid change. Hormones induce physical changes to sexual organs, and changes in physical size and strength. These changes are accompanied by powerful feelings, not only as a direct result of circulating hormones, but also as a consequence of the alterations in psychic balance which come from changes in how young people feel about themselves – for example, from the knowledge of being stronger and being able to conceive or father a baby. These biologically induced developments interact strongly with infantile feelings, so that the young person's fantasies about themselves and their bodies are given a powerful new context. Sometimes these are a great relief: for example, a girl's breast development and menstruation may confirm that she will be able to be a mother after all, and help to overcome depressive fantasies of being damaged and infertile. At other times, extreme anxiety is produced as a result of a merging of frightening infantile fantasies and sexual maturity. Those whose defences against helplessness are based on powerful, omnipotent fantasies may be quite terrified when their physical capacities allow them to act out a murderous fantasy. Or they find that the new circumstances of adolescence come with a sense of the past repeating itself.

> A 15-year-old girl cut herself badly after her first boyfriend dropped her. Later she revealed that her parents' marriage had begun to deteriorate during her infancy, culminating in her father leaving when she was four. In fact her parents were reconciled, and by this time had a happy marriage. However, it became clearer that her own fears about her parents' past unstable marriage, and her belief in her part in it, resulted in a catastrophic identification with her mother when an upsetting but entirely normal event in her social development took place.

The other context of adolescence is that the developmental thrust is towards moving from a state of dependence on parents to inter-dependence on others – ultimately towards sexual partnerships and the acquisition of a capacity to be a parent. There are of course, many fluctuations, but all these developments create powerful surges of contradictory feelings between dependence and independence, which, for those who are vulnerable, can manifest themselves as unbearable anxieties, which can lead to drastic defences.

In adolescence, unbearable feelings are frequently followed by action. The whole process of experiencing feelings, processing them and working through them is frequently replaced by an enactment. The girl who cut herself did not at that time remember her father leaving home or her mother's unhappiness, but when her boyfriend left her she enacted both the father who wounded and the mother who was wounded. It was only later, in the context of an assessment interview, that it was possible for her to bring her capacity to think about her emotional experiences and to connect past and present. This type of enactment, based on rapid projective identification of unprocessed experience is common to most adolescents. But in those at risk it is usually more extreme, and is associated with issues of death, destructiveness and damage in which guilt is a strong feature.

Thus, suicide in adolescence is not an act of self-euthanasia. It is an irrational act based on the very primitive idea that a psychological problem will be solved by the physical act of ending one's life. This may be for a variety of motives: killing off an unbearable part of the self; destroying a destructive internal object; finding peace to escape from persecutors. It is most unlikely that a clear consideration that death really seems to be the best way out is the explanation.

> A young man whom I worked with for several years, who had made many serious suicide attempts, told me once that he imagined jumping out of a window and flying away, leaving his battered and scarred body to fall to the ground. This was not an ordinary religious belief, but a delusion that he could solve his terrible internal state by creating a split between two parts of himself.

When we are faced with assessing a young person who may be at risk, one of the first tasks is to try and establish their story. Where are they developing mentally? What are their main preoccupations? And how are they dealing with them? Sometimes one can get a sense of this by a thoughtful discussion, often by a consideration of their behaviour; but central to any assessment, and indeed treatment, is an exploration of the relationship which develops between the assessing therapist and the patient. The way in which a professional is regarded – whether as potentially helpful, or with suspicion, or perhaps with indifference – gives some indication of the young person's internal capacity to use help – the quality of the internal parents. This may bear a close relationship to actual parents, past and present, though it may not.

Containment in adolescence

Part of adolescent development is the revival of the importance of containing parental figures. The other side of all the acting-out which goes on – which, as I mentioned, was closely related to the increased use of projective identification in adolescence – is that the target of many of these projections is the parents themselves. This is like a revival of the infantile situation in the very different circumstances of adolescence. What is similar in babies and adolescents is the intensity of feeling, which those close to both babies and adolescents are asked to bear. It is the subjection to painful projections that can make aspects of parenting adolescents so difficult at times. Sometimes, it feels as though all the unwanted feelings, hopelessness, incompetence and fear on the one hand, and responsibility and worry without the power to go with it on the other, are left with the parents. Yet just as it is impossible to be unscathed by parenting a baby – babies require this of us – so it is that a part of normal adolescent development is that parents are often worried and uncomfortable. This is one of the reasons why the circumstances for children in care are so difficult. Not only do they have a past history of disturbance, making them more vulnerable, but they are often deprived of parental figures who feel a special obligation to help them in these ways.

When adolescents are assessed, professionals often find themselves in a parental type of role, in receipt of these projections. This is uncomfortable, and at time unnerving, but it is also very informative, and enables them to get a feel of what is going on.

In normal adolescence, there is a fluctuation between the need to use parents as temporary recipients of projections and the ability to take on these functions and to be more independent. Maturation involves the gradual taking over of the function by the young person. It is a regulatory process which allows the more disturbed parts of the personality to be managed, without causing too much danger to the person themselves and those around them. Bion often used the analogy of detoxification. In adolescents, it is the more destructive and disturbed parts of the personality that can lead to states of mind in which there is a risk of self-harm when they take control. If there is an internalised capacity to manage these parts of the self, something that will either take control and overrule the destructiveness, or know when external help is needed, such as a parent or friend, then even quite dangerous states can be managed.

Thus, a crucial question in assessing suicidal risk after an act of self-harm is to assess the presence in the patient of a capacity to care for and help themselves. Do they have evidence of a good internal object and a wish to turn to it? If a young person has taken an overdose, what did they do next? Did they simply go to bed, indicating that they abandoned themselves to a murderous situation? Or did they go and tell someone, who could take them to hospital, indicating that there is some presence in them of an internal parent, temporarily silenced, who can care about them and make sure that they are helped?

As in any assessment, an examination of the quality of internal containment is crucial, and can be arrived at by exploring the quality of the young person's relationship, both to themselves and to others. To what extent do they show concern or even interest in their actions? Do they see themselves as a cause for concern? Do they have the capacity to have an overview of themselves – to see their own plight? It may be that such ideas are around, but more in a projected form – for example, they might complain: 'My mother [or my boyfriend] keeps asking me if I am all right.' In this situation, where the responsibility is projected, the risk is greater, because more is expected of another person; but often there is a very careful unconscious selection of a helpful object or a deep knowledge that a parent will carry the anxiety. An assessment of this capacity to select an object who will care for them, or alternatively to choose an unhelpful or unresponsive object (sometimes repeating infantile situations), is crucial.

A young woman in therapy, prone to wild acting-out and suicidal behaviour, reported to her therapist before a holiday break that she had been driving her car with her boyfriend and had deliberately driven it into the path of an on-coming lorry. The boyfriend had grabbed the wheel and steered the car to safety. The therapist was naturally very concerned, and in discussing this in supervision had tried to weigh up the risks. On the face of it, this suggested a young woman in an extremely dangerous state of mind, who seemed to be at risk of killing both herself and her boyfriend. Her past history had included many self-destructive acts – sometimes literally suicidal, like taking overdoses, and sometimes acts of a more symbolic kind, like getting herself repeatedly thrown out of school and wrecking her education (she was very bright). She seemed to be caught up internally, and to a lesser extent in her current external life, with a seductive and destructive father, with whom she formed a collusive alliance against a denigrated and weak mother. This recent episode had come in the context of some good work in the therapy and the presence of a long-suffering and essentially good boyfriend who was not at all like the father. The countertransference of the therapist had been very intense, and she was familiar with the emotional pressure that this patient put her under.

In weighing up the risk, the crucial questions seemed to be: Was this a communication both of a dangerous state of mind, but also of a presence of a part of her, represented internally by the boyfriend who would take her out of the path of danger? Could this be seen as a communication to the therapist, as well as an attack on her? An important consideration was how she had imparted this material to her therapist in the session. Had it been in a cut-off or triumphant manner? If so, this would have supported the view that she was more in the control of something cruel and destructive that wished to terrify her therapist, just as her boyfriend had been terrified. On the other hand, was there more desperation and anxiety in her tone? This would suggest a more internalised insight that recognised her dangerous state and a wish to be helped.

The decision the therapist took was that, although it was difficult to be sure, there was enough of the patient who had brought this dangerous state to her for help; the patient herself had indeed been shaken by what she had done. This allowed the therapist to feel that she could afford to wait, and to go on assessing whether the patient was coming out of a crisis before the break in her therapy. The weighing-up of whether waiting is helpful, or simply avoiding the necessity to act and therefore dangerous, is always a crucial and difficult decision. Fortunately, in this case it did prove to be the right decision, and the patient, having communicated the danger and felt that she had been heard, survived the break without further suicidal behaviour.

Writing in a *British Medical Journal* publication on Clinical Risk Management, Lipsedge (1995) notes the danger of relying too much on a cross-sectional rather than a longitudinal approach to the assessment of risk-management. He emphasises the importance of developing a sense of history about patients' behaviour, as well as being prepared to repeat assessments.

One of the features of this example is that the countertransference of the therapist was very active. She was full of anxiety, and one could see this as the patient mobilising her objects and filling them with projections which were therefore finding their target. This does not mean there was no risk of suicide, but it does imply an active relationship going on, both externally between the patient and her objects (including her therapist) and internally between different parts of herself – for example, the boyfriend representing a more responsible parenting side of her.

One capacity which was clearly demonstrated was the ability to enter into a relationship in which intense interaction could take place. A relationship in which the seeking of an object to project into and achieve a response was possible.

Some of the most worrying and dangerous young people are those in whom this capacity is markedly impaired. Many such young people do not become professionals. Some of those who commit suicide without ever having sought help probably come into this category. Not surprisingly, when such people do reach us, they are very difficult to assess, and may not know themselves that they are at risk. We get some clues of their impairment from their history of unpredictable, dangerous behaviour. Often this is not accompanied by distress – or at least we cannot get access to, or contact with, a distressed part of themselves. Such young people often have histories of deprivation and disturbed early relationships, which may include sexual abuse. What we meet at assessment is someone who may feel very untrusting, and who is therefore very difficult to engage in a cooperative dialogue. This quality of relationship produces a very difficult countertransference because we cannot use our usual sensitivity as a guide to where the young person is. It may emerge that their means of coping does not involve an idea of being cared for, but instead are based on being in the grip of a more ruthless and omnipotent type of relationship, which often appears to promise to care for them, but in fact is quite murderous, especially if there is any question of disloyalty in it.

> A girl of 14 was referred by her doctor with a history of a serious suicide attempt a year previously, followed some months later by her drinking a whole bottle of vodka, for which she was also hospitalised. She had broken off treatment at another unit and was refusing to be seen with her parents. Indeed, she did not want her parents to know about her referral to us.

A request for the parent not to know of the referral is not uncommon, and, apart from the legal issue of consent to treatment, raises diagnostic questions. Why has the young person requested that her parents be excluded? It is a sign of an impaired relationship with the parents, but what does it mean? Is there a wish to deny the need for parents? Or is it a sign that the parents are mistrusted, perhaps for good reasons. The problem, of course, is that often one just does not know at this stage; and an even more important consideration must be how to engage with the young person in a way that will allow an assessment and treatment to take place. We understood from the doctor that the parents were very concerned about Paula, but felt helpless; and we decided to see her on her own, as she wanted, but we insisted that her parents should know of the referral to us; and we planned to see them once we had engaged with Paula. We knew that Paula's sister had died three years previously, from an 'accidental' drug overdose, and that Paula herself was behaving in a wild, out-of-control way, which was terrifying but paralysing her parents.

During her first assessment session, her therapist reported as follows:

> "Paula is a small, pretty girl with streaked hair who looks both younger and older than her age at the same time. During most of the session she was willing to answer questions, but offered very little information about herself. She quickly withdrew almost as if in a fog and she frequently yawned. When she went to the A&E department she was surprised when they said she could have died if she had come half-an-hour later. She had taken close to seventy paracetamol tablets. It was chilling to hear her talk about her suicide attempt with no emotion or meaning to it."

Paula's disturbing detachment from both the therapist and from her own dangerous behaviour was very striking. The therapist found that she had to work hard on herself during the sessions to remain concerned and appropriately anxious rather than be caught up in what seemed to be a defence against despair, which took the form of a cut-off and disinterested state. When the therapist could hold on to her sense of tragedy with this girl (and of course with her sister's death, which had no space to be spoken of at this stage) there would be moments when Paula would come more to life. However, during the therapist's four-session assessment, she took a planned one-week holiday. During that week Paula took another large overdose and was hospitalised.

It seemed most likely that her sense of being dropped by the therapist was behind the overdose, but, not surprisingly, there was nothing else that Paula conveyed that gave any indication of her attachment to the therapist or any idea of what had been in her mind when she took the overdose. When these things were pieced together, it was possible gradually to build up a picture of a process at work which could give some sense of Paula's actions. Paula seemed to 'think' and communicate almost entirely through her actions – she could communicate depression and despair, but only by taking an overdose which might then give others, if not herself, some knowledge of what had been in her mind at the time. We suspected that the loss of her sister had had a profound effect on her as well as on her parents; but instead of being able to mourn her she seemed to be in a manic identification with her. The desperation was apparent to her helpless parents and those around her. She seemed to be pushing into them feelings of helplessly watching something wildly and dangerously destroying their life. In this way, the pain of the loss of the sister could be inferred, but at the same time with a sense that this was not just a communication, but a very dangerous identification which might well end with her losing her life and her parents losing another child.

This provisional hypothesis was used to provide the basis for thinking about how to complete her assessment and form a treatment plan. With such a dangerous disturbance, including the risk of dangerous acting out, inpatient treatment was obviously indicated. But Paula was adamantly against this. Compulsory admission certainly does have a place in an acute situation, but in the circumstances of Paula's suicidal behaviour, which was ongoing and intermittent, this did not seem to be the solution. In addition, she liked her school and seemed to be well supported there. It was decided to set up a plan of weekly sessions with a psychotherapist, together with at least three weekly appointments with a psychiatrist to evaluate her mental state and supervise her antidepressant medication. Her mother was given charge of these drugs. Her parents were also seen regularly.

With this structure, despite one more slightly weaker suicide-attempt, Paula was gradually able to use her sessions to become more open and to talk about her sad feelings behind all the partying, including how she had not been able to protect herself properly, and had been sexually assaulted as a result. Her dangerous behaviour diminished, and although she broke off treatment after nine months, she was in a less dangerous state and was willing to continue her appointments with the psychiatrist. It was not until right at the end of her treatment that she was herself able to speak with feeling about the loss of her sister.

Other types of impaired container-contained relationships may emerge in assessment. Young people with a history of more perverse or abusive experiences often have had prolonged experience of being used as recipients of unwanted projection by others, such as their parents. This seems to be especially pathogenic when it is in the context of violence. Such relationships impair the development of a capacity for self-care, and emerge in adolescence as the presence of impaired relationships with others, abusive peer relationships, and inability to use professional help. Often the experience of being understood does not bring relief for them, as it produces great conflict, and so it's both very difficult to assess them and to set up appropriate treatment programmes. But the more these circumstances can be properly understood, the more it is possible to find ways of making contact with the young person, or to help those who are struggling to help them.

An integrated assessment

An assessment which is conducted in a way that will allow psychodynamic features to emerge is one that needs to be conducted in a relatively unstructured way. Many structured interviews used for empirical research programmes or checklists could be seen to clash with a psychodynamic approach. If too much of the assessment is spent asking the patient rather than listening to them, it will not be possible to 'hear' the subtleties of what lies behind Paula's silence about herself, or the young woman who tried to kill herself and her boyfriend. A checklist of questions can be used as a means of acting out countertransference anxiety. Instead of holding onto feelings of helplessness or worry, asking a series of questions can be a way of not holding onto the anxiety, or properly processing it in order to arrive at a fuller understanding of the patient, and allowing them to feel heard in a deeper way.

On the other hand, to avoid taking a more active part in an assessment which is full of avoidant behaviour can also be a collusion with the patient not to name the risk, something which they may have persuaded those close to them to do. Careful use of standardised questionnaires, such as the Youth Self Report Form (Achenbach 1991) or for older adolescents the Beck Hopelessness Scale (Beck & Steer 1988), can also have a place, as well as being of value for audit and research.

Provided the therapist is aware of the dynamic significance of asking or not-asking, the use of questions in an assessment becomes a sensible and reality-based piece of equipment which can enormously improve the quality – the degree of accuracy – of risk-assessment. It is therefore helpful to have at the back of one's mind a list of risk factors to draw on which can be converted into questions or lines of enquiry when appropriate. No assessment of any young patient should be regarded as complete without the therapist feeling satisfied about the presence or absence of a significant suicidal risk.

The following is a list of risk factors which can be borne in mind:

Preoccupation with themes of death expressed in talking or writing

Expressing suicidal thoughts or threats

Actual suicidal threats or gestures, even in the distant past

Prolonged periods of depression, such as changes in sleeping patterns, too much or too little sleep or sudden extreme changes in weight and eating habits

Withdrawal and isolation from family and friends

A history of prolonged family conflict and instability

Deteriorating academic performance reflected in lower grades, dropping out of lectures and tutorials, and dropping out of school or college activities

Pending disciplinary issues in school or college

A history of severe or prolonged bullying

A history of family suicides

Persistent abuse of drugs or alcohol

Major personality and behavioural changes indicated by excessive anxiety, or nervousness, angry outbursts, apathy, or lack of interest in personal appearance or in any sexual relationships

Recent loss of a close relationship through death or suicide, or a suicide within school or college

Making final arrangements, leaving a 'goodbye' note, drawing up a will, or giving away prized possessions

Telling someone of their state and intentions

Previous suicide attempts

Sudden unexplained euphoria or heightened activity after a long period of depression. The decision to commit suicide is felt as an abandonment of a painful conflict which can actually lift depression

The development of a psychotic illness – schizophrenia is associated with a markedly increased risk of suicide.

Whom to assess?

Similar principles can guide the therapist in trying to decide who should be seen and in what combination. It is essential to establish a setting in which the young person can feel listened to and in which the dynamics can be visible, and that other relevant people in the young person's life (such as parents or social workers) can be heard and involved too, as they can make a vital contribution.

However, it is important that the trust of the young person is not lost; nor the possibility of examining the transference and countertransference situation. Where professionals are working single-handedly, there is no alternative to making the best compromise between being there for the young person and giving space to other involved adults. When it is possible to have a team, even of two, then these tasks can be divided. Whichever way it is used, there will also be important questions of confidentiality. The young person must feel that confidentiality will be respected, but not to the point of allowing a collusion in which suicidal plans are kept from parents or others *in loco parentis*.

Conclusion

An assessment of risk is at best imprecise. It should get as close as it can in establishing what the risks are. However, it is essential to understand that it is also a therapeutic intervention which, when well conducted, will allow both the young person and those concerned for them to feel more understood and therefore to feel less at risk. It is a relationship with the young person and their system which contains anxiety. In these days of increased litigation, and a greater tendency to practise defensively, there is a risk that this valuable intervention can become more obsessional and defensive itself, and thus be less containing. Professionals at the centre of an assessment of risk do carry responsibilities, and can be at risk themselves if they have not conducted their work to adequate standards. But this pressure not to carry and live with some risk needs to be firmly resisted. In this way, an essential dynamic can operate which can both reduce the risk and allow important information about the patient's state of mind to be included in the assessment of risk.

References

Achenbach, T.M. (1991). *Manual for the Youth Self Report Form and 1991 Profile.* Burlington, Vermont: University of Vermont Department of Psychiatry.

Beck, T. &   Steer, R.A. (1988). *Beck Hopelessness Scale Manual.* San Antonio, Texas: Psychological Corporation.

Hawton, K. & Fagg. J. (1988). Suicide and other causes of death following attempted suicide. *Brit.J. Psychiat.* **152**: 349—366.

Hawton, K., Fagg. J., Simkin, S., Bale, E. & Bond, A. (1997). Trends in deliberate self-harm in Oxford 1985—1995. Implications for clinical services and the prevention of suicide. *Brit.J. Psychiat.* **171**: 556—560.

Lipsedge, M. (1995). Clinical risk management in psychiatry In: *Clinical Risk Management* ed. Charles Vincent. London: BMJ Publishing Group.

Acknowledgement

I would like to thank Professor Phil Richardson and Dr. Helen Keiley for their help with the epidemiological and questionnaire references.

Robin Anderson

Chapter 10

Adolescent breakdown

Emanuela Quagliata in conversation with Eglé Laufer

Emanuela Quagliata

Eglé Laufer is an illustrious member of the British Psychoanalytical Society. Born in Vienna to a Hungarian father and an Italian mother, she moved to England at the age of seven. Having graduated in mathematics and physics, she decided to become a psychoanalyst after reading *Wayward Youth,* which had been suggested to her by her mother, a psychiatrist. Authored by August Aichhorn, this book was published in 1925, with a preface by Sigmund Freud, and described work with adolescents at risk in specialized centers.

Eglé completed psychoanalytic training in 1959. In the meantime, in 1955, Moses (Moe) Laufer (1928–2006), born in Canada to Polish parents who had also been born in Canada, moved to London and began his analytic training at the Anna Freud Centre (the Hampstead Clinic). During that period, Anna Freud and other analysts, such as Aichhorn, Bernfeld, Blos, and Erikson, had begun to be interested in the problem of adolescence.

Married in the mid-1950s, Eglé and Moe also created a lifelong collaboration. In addition to clinical practice, they participated in innumerable conferences and seminars in various countries and wrote books that were translated into many languages, among which the best known in Italy is *Adolescence and Developmental Breakdown* (1984). In 1967, together with colleagues, Eglé and Moe founded the Brent Adolescent Centre, the first psychoanalytically oriented center in Great Britain to focus specifically on adolescents. From 1967 until the present day, this institution has been extensively developed, becoming the preferred training location for a great many psychoanalysts.

Eglé became interested in adolescence following a different journey than that of Moses; she had initially worked with women during an early assignment to an obstetric ward at University College Hospital, where a treatment had been introduced that aimed at preventing postpartum psychosis, stemming from the hypothesis that it was necessary to give particular attention to transitional periods, and that it might be possible to identify more vulnerable women during pregnancy.

As Eglé wrote about later on, the *breakdown* after birth essentially related to the mother-neonate relationship – that is, to a rupture in the relationship, and not to a maternal breakdown that could be ascribed to the woman's psychiatric illness. That

DOI: 10.4324/9781003351184-11

initial work with women was of great importance when Eglé contributed to the creation of the Brent Adolescent Centre, because it led her to identify the roots of adolescent conflict in the changing relationship with one's own body, and it gave her a particular sensitivity to the differences between boys and girls along their developmental journeys, in the perception of their own bodies while they were in transformation.

The goal of this conversation is, first of all, to get to know the conception put forward by Eglé and Moe Laufer regarding the developmental *breakdown* in adolescence, or rather in that phase of development (puberty) in which a "rupture" often occur, a breakdown of the psychic structure that until then had constituted the child's sense of identity.

Emanuela   More than forty years have passed since your husband, Moses
Quagliata: Laufer, published an early definition of developmental breakdown
               in 1975.[1] Revisiting that contribution today, to what degree do
               you think it's still current?

Eglé   This is really the first essay that Moses wrote on the subject, but
Laufer: it was the result of many years of our joint work and work with
               colleagues at the Brent Adolescent Centre. The central aspect
               that we were interested in highlighting was the reality and the
               significance of adolescent disturbance.

               What I mean is that the confusion experienced by the adolescent
               must be taken seriously, not disposed of as something that will pass
               sooner or later. To define the nature and extent of the disturbance
               is useful, first of all, to give an idea of the type and severity of
               the crisis taking place. At one time – but unfortunately, it still
               happens today – some adolescents used to receive a diagnosis of
               developmental "breakdown" and were sent to a psychiatric hospital
               because of potential psychosis. At that point, either they were
               discharged in the belief that the crisis had been overcome, or they
               were given a diagnosis of mental insanity. We were worried about
               the consequences that could result, influencing the entire course
               of the adolescent's life. So, Moe and I insisted on the necessity of
               studying psychotic functioning – not just the psychosis as such – to
               try to define its implications on the diagnostic level. This led to our
               definition of developmental *breakdown*: that is, a crisis characterized
               by an interruption of the normal developmental journey. Adolescence
               is a process of development that involves the body and the mind,
               in the course of which the young person must come to the point of
               defining him-/herself as a man or a woman. What does this mean for
               that person? Today more than ever, we see the necessity of affirming
               these aspects, because the risk always exists of not seeing adolescence
               as a developmental process and of viewing the pathology as
               something fixed. On the contrary, it is essential to remember that the
               breakdown occurs in the context of a normal developmental process.

Beyond this, there is also another aspect to keep in mind, which pertains to Moe's early experiences as a social worker, and that is that people often do not realize the seriousness of certain events. Suppose that the mother dies.... One imagines that in six months, the adolescent will be over this, will have overcome the problem. In general, there is no idea of what development is or of the existence of a process that began in early infancy and that will necessarily be affected by contemporary events; there is no idea of the consequences for future development of a trauma such as the one mentioned. We say "it will pass" even in the face of a suicide attempt.

EQ: In this regard, another of your concerns was the importance of early intervention. Moe wrote in 1997:

"Our current knowledge of the mind allows us to say that many serious disturbances and breakdowns do not arise in a vacuum, but have a very specific meaning in the person's life.... The period of adolescence, that is, from thirteen to about twenty or twenty-one years, [is] perhaps the only occasion when a disabling mental disturbance can be prevented" (pp. 75–76).

EL: Indeed, normal development can be arrested, and thus early intervention must take place immediately after puberty begins so that it can be unblocked, so to speak, restoring the developmental process. The first case of adolescent breakdown that Freud (1901) observed was that of 18-year-old Dora. I had worked as a psychoanalyst in an obstetrics department without being paid since I wasn't a doctor (I wanted to graduate in medicine like my mother, but I was busy with a small child and my studies would have taken too much time away from him). In the hospital, I had met many 16- or 17-year-old girls who had to decide whether to abort or give up the baby for adoption. If they chose to go forward with the pregnancy, I followed them regularly to prevent a postpartum crisis. In these young mothers, crises were very frequent.

Moe and I were especially busy with preventing suicides, which at that time was still considered a crime. During that period, Moe was training at the Anna Freud Centre and had taken into supervision the case of a 17-year-old who had attempted suicide. I had never heard of suicide among young people; it was completely unknown to me. When we began to study the problem, we looked for warning signs in adolescents who had tried to take their own lives and who were willing to talk with us about it. We succeeded in getting funds to launch a research project on six cases of adolescent survivors of a suicide attempt. In working with these patients, the hypothesis of a developmental "breakdown" emerged; they did not talk explicitly about the hatred they felt toward their own bodies, but we understood that what they were attacking in attempting suicide was the body itself. From that research, we began to elaborate the concept of developmental *breakdown*, which must not be confused with a simple nervous breakdown. Suicide is the extreme form of breakdown; it is the only way to regain control over what is happening: to destroy the body because the enemy is the body – just as it is, furthermore, in all other self-harming behaviors.

It wasn't a simple undertaking. At the Brent Centre, we offered five sessions a week without charge, but parents and psychiatrists wanted to return the boys and girls to school as soon as possible. I don't think it was a form of denial, but rather the fact that all the workers (key doctors, social workers, teachers) were very alarmed at the idea of having contact with those children, of keeping them nearby; their main preoccupation was to reinsert them into the flow of normal life. But a suicide attempt must in some way be understood and integrated.

EQ: This is a very interesting point on the central focus on integration. You made a distinction between the libidinal body linked with the memory of early mother-child interactions, and the body image which is based on sensory experience. These two experiences should be integrated in what you defined the the body as an internal object. When this integration doesn't occur the adolescent resume to hatred of one's own body and extreme solutions.

You now also stress the importance for the professionals to understand and integrate the breakdown and suicidal experience of the adolescent.

On many occasions, you and Moe have emphasized the difficulty that parents and clinicians encounter in facing the serious aggression that the adolescent may direct toward his or her own body, feeling it to be an enemy. For example, Moe wrote: "In adolescence, *breakdown* has a very precise meaning and must always be taken seriously. This means that the adolescent who attempts suicide, who chooses to resort to drugs to alter his mental life, who is pushed to physically attack others, who at school has a violent and threatening attitude, has lost contact with his mental life and is responding to creations of his own mind (which also contain hatred for the self and for his own body). He is subjected to enormous pressure at school, in his work, or among friends, to accept this behavior as normal, but it is a normality that contains the seeds of the adolescent's self-destruction." (1997, p. 77)

EL: The point is something understood to be self-destructive. Here we are speaking of the image that is projected from the external world onto the young person's body. This is not normality. Normal is defensive behavior; we are all capable of it, but in the case of adolescents, it's different because there is something else at play: adolescents make use of extreme defenses to deny the existence of a body that escapes their control and is therefore scary. The wish to destroy the enemy is thus defensive. At a conscious level, one believes the body is under control, but the body can reveal itself in adolescence to be an uncontrollable enemy. For example, if you think you are ugly and you want to be pretty, the defense you will turn to is cosmetic surgery. But the image projected from the outside comes from the real world, and it is exactly such an image – when it doesn't agree with what the adolescent feels – that represents the object of his hatred.

EQ: The *breakdown* in the course of development is accompanied, then, by a mental break with the world: consequently, one's own mental creations prevail over what happens in the external world. Do you assign a defensive function to a psychotic functioning of this type? The defensive strategies mobilized would have the goal of drastically limiting the relationship with the changing body, blocking a sexuality experienced as terrifying.

EL: Yes. When the adolescent feels he cannot control what happens in his body, he withdraws from the world. But the reality he tries to deny is inherent in his body. Wherever he finds himself reckoning with this reality, continually called to mind by the external world, he drastically distances himself. He has the feeling that the threat comes from outside, and so he withdraws from school and from his family; there are adolescents who shut themselves up in their rooms for months, sometimes even years. I had a patient who was convinced that her friends at school were aware of when she had her menstrual periods; for this reason, she decided to stay home in bed for two years running.

Today I would say that pubertal changes can provoke a *breakdown* if the adolescent cannot integrate the relationship with his new body into an appropriate sense of reality – that is, to modify that relationship in line with his sense of reality. In other words, when the adolescent can't let go of his childhood body, the one that is still tied to the maternal body; it is necessary that he detach from it, accept the physical changes that have taken place, and in this sense maintain contact with external reality.

The trauma of puberty resides in having a body that the adolescent may have perhaps desired ever since he was a child; now, however, the situation is different because it is no longer a fantasy: his sexualized, adult body could actually allow him to kill his father and impregnate his mother. For this reason, we speak of "trauma"; puberty is traumatic because it radically changes the relationship with reality.

I don't think that this conceptual picture is mistaken, but the way in which Moe describes it would have to be elaborated. This is not about changing the conception itself, but today, having used it for some time, I would formulate it in a slightly different way. What needs to be said is that the relationship with reality must proceed at the same rate as the relationship with the body; to deny the change means rejecting the new body and wanting to remain a child. It is certainly a break in the relationship with reality, but with a reality defined specifically in relation to the body.

The consequences of the *breakdown* can be quite varied. From seeking refuge in isolation, detaching oneself from external objects, to the refusal to go on living, from the idea that to resolve all problems one must destroy one's own physically mature body, to decisively breaking with reality and the consequent emergence of a psychotic organization. One must never think of this as a passing crisis, but rather as the serious result of the adolescent's reaction to a body that he hates and of which he wishes to rid himself. In this sense, given that it sets the stage for the real objective of preventing normal development, it constitutes a break in the normal developmental trajectory.

But, returning to the definition of developmental *breakdown,* today I would put more emphasis on the adolescent's relationship with his own body than with external reality. The adolescent cannot fully accept having a different body, nor all that he can do with it in relation to the external world, with respect to the mother as a prohibited object and the father as a rival whom he is now capable of killing. Integration of the new body and the new bodily image into the mind is a developmental process that can collapse, and it is for this reason that we speak of a "developmental *breakdown.*" Moe always wrote "breakdown" in quotation marks because it is a very specific type of break.

EQ: Speaking of the impact that the physical and sexual maturity of puberty can have on some adolescents, I think you introduced a major reference to loss and mourning. In the 1991 article published in the *International Journal of Psychoanalysis,* you wrote that puberty can represent the loss of an idealized bodily image, which until that moment permitted the child to feel loved and secure. Anna Freud's writing about this is excellent.

EL: Yes, certainly, I did speak of loss and mourning. It is important to mention what Anna Freud wrote about this, explaining that the work of mourning is an integral part of the developmental process. In this case, mourning pertains to the loss of the childhood body and is translated into a sense of being without something, of resistance to separation, because the relationship between the child's body and that of the mother is still present.

But there is also another aspect: that is, that the adolescent can perceive his new sexually mature body as disgusting, and he expects that others will also see it as such. For the girl whom I spoke of earlier, the one convinced that everyone at school knew when she had her menstrual period, this was the reality. The construction of an alternative reality is a defense against a self-harming attack, because the other option would be to attack one's own body. Rather than physically destroy the self, the adolescent turns to a psychotic-type organization that gives rise to a series of acting out behaviors: adolescents who shut themselves off in their rooms or who categorically refuse to go to school. I remember a patient at our center who wanted to take a trip to India (like many young people at that time), and there, stretched out on the roof of a train station, she watched people who passed by underneath. For her it was a great relief that other people couldn't see her while she could see them from above. Instead of making friends, of strengthening relationships, she had escaped somewhere far away, and her defense was the roof of an Indian station from which she could see others instead of being seen. From this voluntary exile, she came to the Brent Centre and asked us how she might be able to make some friends. She was fighting against the temptation to isolate herself and was battling the conviction that the other, the object of her desire, would hate and scorn her.

EQ: Regarding the adolescent's effort to disengage from childhood experiences, what is your view of the relationship between the adolescent experience and the childhood relationship with the parents? In your opinion, how do the separation and individuation processes proceed?

EL: Freud considered childhood relationships in terms of the oedipal complex. The first conflicts pertaining to the fact of being male or female can be located in the oedipal realm. All that is reactivated at puberty, when the body predominates. And the way in which the Oedipus is resolved is critical. The adolescent developmental phase is a repetition of the oedipal one, which must now integrate the fact of having a sexualized body. It is based on this, in our opinion, that homosexuality harkens back to the oedipal complex, resolved with the conclusion that the mom prefers you as a little boy or little girl. The relationship with the mother is very special, and the relationship that mother has with father is used to attack the maternal figure: "Mom doesn't want me, I'll go to Dad."

The fantasy regarding the body (the body as an internal object, or rather the internalized image of how the mother would like her child to be and that would make him worthy of love) is different from the reality of the body. Up until what point the adolescent manages to integrate the reality of his own body is what distinguishes normal development from pathological development. One can create the object in fantasy (and this contributes to the central masturbatory fantasy): to create the object that desires you each time that you want it to.

It is always important to emphasize the theme of the relationship with one's own body and the internalized bodily image – for example, in the particular case of the self-harming by girls who inflict cuts and wounds on themselves. This behavior, in our belief, is an expression of the fact that they are rejecting their own bodies. One time, in speaking with a young girl, I asked her what she wanted when she wounded herself, and it clearly emerged that this was an attack on the body that she hated, that she didn't accept.

When Moe speaks of "mental creations," he is referring to "fantasies." The fantasies are an attempt to integrate an awareness of having a particular body. These adolescents fantasize that no one wants their body any longer, and so they hate it; the fantasy is of being able to modify it, to force it to change in a way that they can have it as they want it. If the body is no longer desired by anyone, the adolescent identifies with the fantasy of being able to deny what he has and of having what he wants. In the case of plastic surgery, the adolescent is more aware of it and may even threaten to kill himself if he cannot get the intervention that can transform his body into something that he will like better.

EQ: Your concept of central masturbatory fantasy (1986) describes a fantasy that typically emerges around puberty, potentially existing alongside the adolescent's masturbatory fantasies and behaviors. You highlight how the central masturbatory fantasy is structured during childhood and, as in Freudian's model, childhood is viewed as encompassing various forms of oedipal and pre-oedipal erotic satisfaction. Moments of crisis are inevitable, considering that the adolescent period is as you say "in the best of cases stressful, and at times frightening." Parents, clinicians, and educators ask themselves how it is possible to define the difference between stress, desperation, or the sense of impotence that fall within normal development, and the analogous phenomena that are instead signs of a *breakdown*. In your 1997 work, some points are listed to describe what is necessary so that the adolescent doesn't feel psychically abandoned – do you consider these to still be current?

EL: Today I would formulate these five points in the following terms: First, the adolescent can feel that he no longer needs his parents because he has enough friends and no longer totally depends on the parents for approval and self-esteem, but can instead count on his capacity to make friends. The central issue is not only to detach from the parents, but also to be able to make friends, to establish relationships with new objects.

Second, due to his physical development, the adolescent may feel guilty or ashamed of certain intimate thoughts or feelings originating in his new body, but that doesn't prevent him from enjoying it or from seeking relationships that help him maintain contact with those feelings and thoughts.

Third, sometimes the adolescent may have thoughts that he is ashamed of and that worry him, since to him they seem tied to some kind of sexual anomaly. Owing to this conviction, sometimes these thoughts appear during masturbation, but the adolescent is aware of being able to control them and is not overwhelmed by them.

Fourth, he is disturbed by the fact that he can't repress certain feelings that from time to time overwhelm him. He expels them from his mind and then suddenly becomes agitated because he notices he hasn't forgotten them at all, but he feels relieved when he discovers that forgetting them is possible. The adolescent completely ignores what will happen in the future, and this is another way of saying that he is not overly frightened. The *breakdown* happens only when the mind is overwhelmed by unacceptable ideas and feelings.

Fifth, despite feelings of emptiness and anxiety experienced in the process of detachment from parental figures of the past (I wouldn't call them the parents of the past, however, but the parents *tout court*), he carries with him from childhood a sufficient supply of love for himself to permit him to look ahead to the future, to a future that can perpetuate what he feels is good in himself and in his parents.

All this means that for narcissistic investment, one must count on one's self and not on one's parents. In other words, without being aware of it, the adolescent who develops normally can see the future as a time in which he will succeed in freeing himself from the unavoidable aggression toward his parents, going forward with the internal freedom to excuse them for the inevitable disappointments that they have inflicted on him.

All in all, I can only reaffirm that, in adolescent conflict, the sexually mature body always comes into play as one of the main sources of anxiety and feelings of anomaly, madness, or unworthiness. Whatever they do, these adolescents are tormented by self-accusations and by the idea of being abnormal. They often convince themselves that these creations of their mind are real – for example, the boy convinced that he has an ugly nose, or the girl who believes she has breasts that are too small or too big. Sometimes they can persuade themselves that others hate them, and therefore they try to destroy or damage the developing body that they believe is responsible for such persecution. Obviously, the adolescent doesn't realize that he is reacting to his own fantasies, and in moments of desperation, he believes that his experience is real. But the experiences *are* real; there is real anxiety for the young girl convinced that her only problem is that her breasts are too small, not her timidity or the fact of feeling she is unloved. Not even the boy who thinks he has an ugly nose has the slightest doubt that this is his problem, convinced as he is of being surrounded by hostile critics who make fun of him.

EQ: This seems the crucial point...

EL: It is impossible to convince them that their nose is not too long, or their breasts are not too small, and that it isn't true that there's nothing to do but have them surgically modified. It is as though the only alternative to destruction of one's own body is to force one's parents to arrange a surgical procedure to change it. The adolescent insists, and the parents are afraid. The adolescent doesn't accept the surrender to his own body, over which he has no control; the body becomes a constant source of persecution.

EQ: I'd like to go back to the importance of identifying these disturbances and intervene in a timely way, using Moe's words (1997):

"The sense of urgency that is often silently present in our work with disturbed adolescents is born of the awareness that, if in this phase one allows the crisis to run its course, it can destroy the person's emotional future, with the result that their adult life is irredeemably ruined, becoming a compromise, aimed at fighting an unknown enemy installed in the mind. The adolescent *breakdown* doesn't stop at the end of adolescence, but goes on to take over the internal world and the social relationships with the external world. In the best of cases, the result is a damaged or distorted relationship with the self and with others, but often the tragic consequence of an untreated *breakdown* in adolescence is a definitive mental illness, which inevitably involves a rupture in the relationship with the world."

EL: Yes, it is essential to stop a pathology that, if left to itself, would certainly end up destroying the person's emotional life. The adolescent feels incapable of reversing the process, overwhelmed as he is by the changes in his body over which he no longer has control. His mind and his body are now the enemy. Because of this, it is very important that the adolescent goes to therapy, and I agree with Moe when he writes that with our knowledge today of the human mind, it is not permissible to not intervene; we know that the *breakdown* has a particular meaning for the individual in question, and we also begin to have an idea of the specific contribution that the experiences of adolescence can carry forward to adult life, in a constructive sense or a destructive one. In health and in illness, adolescence is the period in which the relationship with the self and with the external world is fixed and becomes irreversible, while the development of mental health or illness assumes a more definite and predictable character in the presence of a sexually mature body.

EQ: Do you think that adolescents and parents have changed a lot in the last twenty years?

EL: During the period in which we wrote about these issues, we knew much less about them. We didn't even know that some adolescents cut themselves and attack their bodies in various ways. All this was kept totally secret. What counts is that the therapist, the parents, or whoever else knows recognizes the signs. In speaking with parents, we wanted them to understand, without terrifying them, that something can be done, that the *breakdown* is not inevitable, and that with appropriate intervention the danger can be overcome. The parents who deny the problem are those who fall into crisis, sometimes because they can't manage to come to grips with the fact that their son has become a sexualized being, or because of the guilty feelings that constitute a constant source of anxiety. Many adolescents come to psychotherapy because they are afraid; they know they have lost control of their thoughts and actions, and they no longer feel in charge of their own life. If we allow ourselves to flee from a serious disturbance because the adolescent can't tell us about it, or because we can't allow ourselves to listen to what he says, we will have lost an opportunity that may not present itself again.

EQ: Can you tell me something about your work with parents?

EL: I think this is an important factor, but I would pose the question in a different way: up to what point can the adolescent be protected? If you're the parent of a girl who tried to kill herself, it is certainly necessary that the therapist meet you and speak with you. And it isn't easy to find the right words to explain that an event of this type doesn't arise out of nothing. When Moe discussed the creation of the center with Anna Freud, he explained that we wanted a place where adolescents could feel treated on their own, without the parents or siblings interfering with the analyst. Moe saw the adolescent before the parents, and only with the adolescent's permission did he speak with them. Calls home were limited to saying, "May I speak with your son?" Knowing him, I think that in speaking with parents, he didn't go into detail but confined himself to emphasizing how important it was to take the treatment seriously, explaining that psychoanalysis is a complex intervention and not like taking a pill – for example, an antidepressant that treats only the symptom. Parents have to better understand what is happening. We wrote that there are many disturbed adolescents, scared and full of shame, but who are nonetheless capable of responding to an intervention that speaks to their internal world and their suffering. Moe was very careful and respectful in showing the parents that he could understand their problem. He avoided criticizing them in any way, because he absolutely did not want them to feel ashamed or guilty for not having noticed the situation. It is a very rare quality, but it is the way he behaved, with great gentleness and consideration.

EQ: **In conclusion**, I would like to talk about prevention. You and Moses founded the Brent Adolescent Centre, where adolescents could go and receive even intensive psychoanalytic support free of charge, a unique place of extraordinary importance in the prevention of adolescent mental disorders. How do you explain the difficulty that many professionals, psychologists, psychiatrists and not only parents or teachers, encounter in intercepting and understanding the early signs of mental disorder in young people?

EL: I think that if we are not in touch with the meaning that our own adolescent years had for us, and with the meaning of the answers or compromises that we ourselves have found in coming to terms with that period, our work with the disturbed or ill adolescent loses meaning and is resolved in compromise solutions, leading us to minimize the extent of the danger. The phrase "with time it will pass" becomes an excuse for our compromises and our frustrations. In that way, the "blind spots" of our life can produce serious consequences for our work with disturbed adolescents. If we can't manage to take seriously what they are trying to tell us, we lose the opportunity to help them heal a break with the world.

Of one thing we are convinced: any discussion around mental health, illness, and the adolescent's developmental crises will sound authentic only if those of us who work with adolescents are able to revisit our own personal stories: our disappointments and suffering, fears and madness, concerns about sexual anomalies – in general, the way in which we have coped with these problems and the resolutions we have found in the course of our mental development. If we cannot use what we've learned to give meaning to our adolescent life, then certain aspects of what we have discussed will remain, in the best of cases, a mere intellectual exercise, stripped of the conviction of being able to provide essential help to the adolescents with whom we work.

EQ: Thank you!

Note

1 Laufer, M. (1975). *Adolescent Disturbance and Breakdown.* Penguin Books.

Bibliography

Aichorn (1925). First German edition 1925: Verwahrloste Jugend In August Aichhorn, Verwahrloste Jugend, 5-6, Leipzig Vienna and Zurich: Internationaler Psychoanalytischer Verlag. English ed. Wayward Youth 1935 The Viking Press.

Freud, Anna (1957). Adolescence. [In *Works,* Vol. 2.] *Selected Writings.* Penguin Books.

Freud, Sigmund (1901 [1905]). Fragment of an analysis of a case of hysteria (Dora). *Standard Edition,* 7:1–122.

Laufer, Eglé (1982). Female masturbation in adolescence and the development of the relationship to the body. *International Journal of Psychoanalysis,* 63:295–302.

Laufer, Eglé (1991). Body image, sexuality and the psychotic core. *International Journal of Psychoanalysis,* 72:63–71.

Laufer, Eglé (1997). Some prerequisites of psychoanalytic work with adolescents. *Richard and Piggle,* 5:67–72.

Laufer, Eglé (2005). Le corps comme objet interne. *Adolescence,* 23(2):363–379.

Laufer, Moses (1975). *Adolescent Disturbance and Breakdown.* Penguin Books.

Laufer, Moses, ed. (1995). *The Suicidal Adolescent.* Routledge.

Laufer, Moses, ed. (1997). Defining breakdown. In Moses Laufer *Adolescent Breakdown and Beyond.* Karnac Books.

Laufer, Moses & Laufer, M. Eglé (1984). *Adolescence and Developmental Breakdown: A Psychoanalytic View.* Routledge, 1995.

Glossary

Acting-out An almost magical use of action at the expense of thought. Action cuts off any connection with thought and replaces it. It is a kind of 'short circuit' of psychic functioning, deriving from the internal world which is full of anxiety, and is intolerant of psychic pain.

Analytic bond The relationship established between therapist and patient during psychotherapy. The analytic bond facilitates the conscious and unconscious communications between patient and therapist.

Analytic setting In psychoanalytic therapy, the setting is the space where it is possible to observe the roles and the emotions which are in action between patient and therapist. This enables the therapist to reflect on the patient's internal experiences in what is an almost 'experimental context'. The analytic setting has some specific rules, for example, the therapist does not share personal information and maintains a neutral stance. With adolescent patients, more than with adult ones, these rules can be restrictive and in some cases they might hinder therapeutic work. For this reason, in the work with adolescents, these rules can be modified in order to facilitate the engagement of the patient.

Antisocial acts Violent behaviours stemming both from the subject's internal psychic organization and from the environment. Antisocial acts tend towards denial, the destruction of bonds and the negation of the subjectivity of the other person. Antisocial acts in adolescence tend to lead the adolescent to review and reorganize, in a destructive way, his/her own sense of internal continuity. They provide a defence from the anxiety of one's limitations; the aim is to escape a reality check which is necessary in order to overcome a developmental impasse.

Asceticism A defence mechanism in which the pleasant effects of experiences are eliminated. Gratification comes from renunciation: ascetism is used against pleasure. Its aim is to develop a protection from impulses which, in fantasy, are perceived as dangerous and a source of anxiety.

Attachment Term used to indicate the quality of the bond established between the child and its caregivers. According to John Bowlby, secure attachment is derived from a stable and satisfying relationship. Conversely, if the relationship proves to be a source of uncertainty, hostility, and rejection, the child will resort to an anxious, avoidant, or disorganized attachment style

Body image   The cognition, constantly evolving over time, of one's own body – this is something fundamental for the consolidation of identity. It enables to acquire self-awareness as a real, constant entity in time, as well as to establish relationships. Through body image, the sensory, affective and cognitive apparatus that ensures growth is gradually developed.

Borderline personality disorder   A personality pathology characterized by a marked impairment in psychosocial functioning, pervasive instability of self-image and mood, feelings of emptiness and abandonment, dissociative symptoms, intense and unmotivated anger. It is characterized by a chronic dispersion of identity, where, despite resorting to defence mechanisms (especially splitting, idealization, and devaluation), the capacity for reality testing is not seriously impaired. Furthermore, there is a systematic succession of contrasting feelings of fusion and abandonment, leading to oscillations between states of euphoria and depression. This makes these patients 'stable in their instability'. The reconstruction of the patient's emotional history often shows how these mental organizations are the result of longstanding are the result of longstanding defense mechanism that mantain a psychic equilibrium but meave suffering unchanged. Finally, regarding the understanding and the treatment of borderline patients, it is important to note that the patients' deficit in the capacity to think, or mentalization, is central in this pathology.

Bullying   A series of behaviours in which the roles of the perpetrator and the victim are reinforced over time through intentionally perpetrated acts of bullying. Intentionality refers to the subject's conscious will to perform physical and verbal acts with the aim of causing harm and injuring a specific other.

Confusional states   A state in which the Self or parts of the Self cannot be distinguished appropriately from objects of internal or external reality. Thought processes are confused, as it is a discrimination between good and bad objects.

Countertransference   Countertransference indicates the conscious and unconscious aspects of the therapist's emotional response to the patient. It is an essential tool for therapeutic understanding and communication, it also helps to reveal the mental state of the patient.

Defensive behaviours   Operations used by the Ego to activate defences. They describe the struggle of the Ego to protect itself from dangers (loss of the loved object, loss of the love of the object, disapproval of the Superego) and from the unpleasant affects associated with those dangers.

Denial   A defence process by which the individual 'denies' psychic reality or the importance of figures on which it depends. This is done through devaluation (not recognizing the importance of the other), idealization (denying negative aspects and recognizing only positive ones), triumph, and omnipotence (through control and domination of the other).

Depressive position   A mental state characterized by the integration of split parts, in the Self and Other. This allows the child to recognize how the idealized mother is also the hated mother- it is the same person. Relationships are with whole objects, for whom the child feels love and concern. This leads to feelings of guilt for the harm done in phantasy and to a desire to repair. In the depressive position, love mitigates hatred, feelings of hope and security increase. If the depressive position fails, manic triumph dominates and schizo paranoid modes are reactivated.

Destructive narcissism   A pathological organization characterized by hostility towards relationships and dependence on others. This is in opposition to a different kind of narcissism (libidinal), which is a defence against adverse object relations. According to the psychoanalyst Herbert Rosenfeld, some patients' destructive narcissism manifests itself as a mental state in which the patient idealizes aspects of the Self which are akin to an organized gang structure, led by an omnipotent and omniscient mafia boss, towards whom the patient turns as a source of superior strength. This tyrannical figure allows the patient to live in a state of peace without experiencing envy, dependence, separateness, or need for the other. Destructive narcissism induces the patient to attack the therapist, seen as the object which is meant to nourish vital and needy parts, this pushes the patient towards increasingly serious self-destruction.

Dissociation   The term indicates the exclusion of some mental contents from consciousness. The dissociated elements are not integrated into conscious awareness, memory, and identity. Dissociation can involve thought processes, emotions, sensorimotor functionality, and behaviours.

Drives   According to Freud's drive theory, a drive is an instinctual need that is at the core of any action and behaviour. There are two drives, the life instinct, striving towards self-preservation and pleasure, and the death instinct which stands at the polar opposite. The drives encapsulate aggressive and destructive impulses. Both instinctual drives battle within us, shaping our actions and desires.

Eating disorders (ED)   Manifested through excessive restriction (anorexia nervosa) of food intake or through compulsive binge-eating of large quantities of food (bulimia) or, alternatively, through the alternation between the two, which has become quite common today. The anorexia/bulimia pair constitutes a model of adolescent psychopathology in the struggle against dependency and depressive feelings. ED tend to appear for the first time in adolescence and often continue into adulthood. Psychoanalytic studies have emphasized the notion of the anorectic and/or bulimic thinking rather than the syndrome (that is, a cluster of specific symptoms.) These pathologies centrally involve the body, whose rapid changes in adolescence cannot be controlled. In anorexia, there is a denial of the reality of the body, particularly the sexual body. The body is mortified and leading to what Kestenberg calls 'fasting orgasm'. Alongside this pursuit, there is the phantasy of the idealized body which expresses the need for fusion with a mother whose loss cannot be tolerated.

The anorectic symptom of fasting depends on this fusion and at the same time realizes it, preventing adult sexual maturation and perpetuating the infantile bond with the parent. The body is denied as a sexualized body or as a differentiated body in terms of gender, even if displayed. The body to be nourished, starved, intruded upon bulimically, or denied in terms of sexuality constitutes a third object in the dynamic between the adolescent and the Self, the adolescent and the parents, the adolescent and the peer group.

Ego, Id and Super Ego   Freud believed that human personality has more than a single component. In his theory, he states that a personality is composed of three elements, the Id, the Ego and the Super Ego; they work together to create complex human behaviours. The Id is the basis of sexual and aggressive energy and is largely held in the unconscious. It is driven by the pleasure principle which demands immediate gratification of all desires and needs. If these needs are not satisfied, the result is a state of anxiety or tension. It is the development of the Ego and the Super Ego that allows us to control the Id's basic instincts. The Ego develops from the Id and ensures that its impulses can be expressed in an acceptable manner. The Ego functions in the conscious, preconscious and unconscious mind. It operates on the reality principle, which strives to satisfy the Id's desires in realistic and socially acceptable ways. The reality principle weighs the costs and benefits of an action before deciding to act upon or abandon impulses. The Super Ego is the moral compass of the personality, upholding a sense of right and wrong, values that are initially learned from ones' parents.

Embodied relationship   A relationship in which bodily experience can be represented in the mind of the Other, thus facilitating the development of a coherent sense of Self that is rooted in the body.

Embodiment   It is a term that describes the intrinsic connection between mind and body.

Etiology   In medicine, it is the study of the factors that cause disease. In psychopathology, it explains the variables and reasons why a disorder manifests itself.

Evolutionary breakdown and puberty   A critical event in puberty that has a cumulative effect throughout adolescence, with serious implications on normal adolescent functioning and development. A breakdown brings to a halt the process of integrating the physically mature body and the adolescent's self-representation. This brings an unconscious rejection of the sexual body and a feeling of passivity in relation to the demands that so forcefully come from the body. A breakdown often expresses the adolescent's anxiety and panic in suddenly finding him/herself in possession of a sexually mature body. The effects of a breakdown can become immediately evident around the onset of puberty or later, during adolescence.

Fixation   Arrest of development at an immature level or stage where the creative response to environmental stimuli is interrupted; a 'refusal to grow', generally unconscious, which prevents facing a new psychic organization, a new adaptation.

Functional disorder   As opposed to an organic disorder where there is a measurable change to organs or body systems in a functional disorder there are abnormal symptoms or changes in function but with no measurable organic changes. The cause of a functional disorder cannot be established.

Functional somatic disorder (FSD)   Persistent and widespread somatic symptoms (mainly motor-sensory ones) which do not have an identifiable organic cause. The symptoms cause significant physical and psychological distress in the patient, as well as excessive thoughts and feelings related to the same symptoms.

Idealization   A psychic process that leads to the exaltation of the value and qualities of the object in order to protect from the inability of the fragile Ego to properly internalize a good object which doesn't need to be idealized.

Identification   A psychoanalytic term that designates the process by which a subject assimilates one or more aspects of another individual, modelling oneself on it. With the defensive mechanism of identification, the Ego attempts to escape from a distressing psychic situation by identifying with the object that contains the distress.

Identification with the aggressor   The process through which the individual seeks to escape the attacker's assault and evade the related anxiety of destruction by assuming the same threatening function of the aggressor.

Identity   It is the synthesis of Ego integration that allows one to act as a coherent and stable unit. The basis of the emotional experience of identity lies in perceiving the self as an organized unit differentiated from the surrounding environment. The feeling of identity is related to psychosexual development and relational experience in early childhood. During the upheaval of adolescence, there is the beginning of an internalized identity, different from the one of the parents.

Infant observation   A formative experience introduced by Esther Bick, a British psychoanalyst, in child psychotherapy trainings, starting in 1948. From the 1960s, infant observation was included in the programs of the British Institute of Psychoanalysis. In Italy, this training method has been used since 1976. It involves weekly home observations conducted by students who visit a newborn baby from birth, for two years. In the regular observations, the student observes the newborn in relation to its parents and other family figures (grandparents, siblings, aunts, uncles). The objective of the visits is to identify how the infant's internal world is structured, this is done through a careful observation of the emotional exchanges that occur between the newborn and its primary carers.

Intellectualization   A defence mechanism whereby everything is brought to the realm of rationality, logical thinking and abstraction. Pleasure is understood solely as an intense intellectual activity that leads to playing with ideas; this is done in order to suppress emotions, desires, and needs.

Internal conflict   Conflict occurs when two emotions clash with each other, the fulfillment of one is incompatible with that of the other.

Internal object   A term used in Kleinian vocabulary, indicating an unconscious phantasy of a very early relationship between the self and an object which is felt by the infant to be located in the body. This internalised object can cause discomfort (for example, when the infant is hungry and its tummy hurts) or pleasure (the opposite experience, the infant is fed). The experience of the internal object is deeply dependent on the experiencing of the external object (e.g., mother or father). In this way, internal objects are mirrors of reality.

Internal world   The relationships that the subject entertains with external objects (people and things) that have been internalized, thus becoming 'internal objects'. The internal world is an internal reference scheme through which experience is filtered it is as real as the external world. It is difficult to trace a clear separation between innate and acquired factors involved in the formation of the internal world, but the subjective element that colours the perception of external events is evident.

Introjection   The process by which aspects of the external world and the interactions with it are taken into the internal structure and become part of inner life. According to Kleinian theory, introjection and projection form the basis of the child's mental and emotional development. They contribute to building a secure personality through the experience of having introjected internal good objects, with the consequent experience of an inner sense of goodness, self-confidence, and mental stability.

Introjective identification   The process through which the qualities of the Self are constructed through the phantasy of introjecting objects whose qualities become part of the Self.

Latency   The period between the fifth/sixth year and the onset of puberty. It is characterized by a progressive decline in early instinctual drives, a strengthening of the Ego, and the parallel shift of interest from psychic reality to the external world. The relationship between a child and its parents begins to lose its exclusive character, the child seeks new objects of love and admiration. Latency separates childhood sexual development from the genital organization proper to adolescence: in latency, sexual evolution temporarily slows down with the appearance of feelings such as modesty and privacy.

Libidinal stages of development   Freud suggests that the personality of the child goes through five psychosexual stages: the oral (birth to 1 year) anal (1 to 3 years), phallic (3 to 6 years) latency (6 years to puberty) and genital (puberty to adulthood) During these stages sexual energy/sexual drive (libido) is expressed in different ways and through different body parts.

Mentalization   It is the capacity to reflect on mental states in oneself and in others, combined with the implicit or explicit awareness that these mental states are representations of reality from one of many possible points of view. The term 'mentalization' emerged in psychoanalytic literature in the late 1960s. In the 90' Peter Fonagy and his colleagues applied it to the study of developmental psychopathology within the context of dysfunctional attachment relationships and clinical interventions with parents and children.

Mourning   A process, described for the first time by Freud, that comes after the loss of a loved one, from which the individual gradually manages to detach. This intrapsychic work involves various phases: from a temporary lack of interest in the external world, one gradually moves towards a process of internalizing the loved one through memories which facilitate the acceptance of separation from the lost object. If this slow process is not completed, grief can become pathological and impossible to overcome: in this case normal grief becomes depression.

Narcissistic (pathological) organization   Character structure in which stability does not derive from dependence on reliable parental figures with whom the Self can identify. On the contrary, parts of the Self, seeking good relationships are terrified by bad parts. The latter ones are internally organized in a 'mafia' like gang, dominated by a leader dispensing false information about the external world. Such character structure may serve to ward off fear of chaos, fragmentation, or depressive suffering.

Neurosis   A condition that involves symptoms of stress (depression, anxiety, obsessive behaviour, hypochondria) caused by past conflicts that have been repressed.

Neurotic conversion   A psychological condition that causes symptoms that appear to be neurological, such as paralysis, speech impairment or tremors, but with no obvious or known organic causes.

'No-entry' defensive system   The psychotherapist Gianna Polacco Williams (Int.J.Psych.oanalysis 1997) refers to a 'No-entry syndrome' as a defence system of patients who are hard to reach. Patients suffering from eating disorders often belong to this category. In many of them, there is a specific request not to 'cross the border'; this is due to their difficulty in establishing and internalizing a dependent relationship. This is a defensive system that can develop in early childhood in children who have felt invaded by chaotic and disorganizing anxieties coming from a parent; these anxieties were probably experienced by the helpless child as alien bodies. The function of the 'No-entry syndrome 'is to block any input felt as intrusive and persecutory.

Nosographical   The description of the symptoms and aetiology of a disease.

Object   It is a technical term that, in the context of psychoanalytic object relations theory, indicates a person with whom the subject maintains an emotional relationship. An external object is a person from external reality, an internal object has been introjected and is part of the internal world.

Oedipal complex   As Oedipus in Sophocles' Oedipus Rex, human beings find themselves in a situation of conflict, both because birth marks a separation from the ideal state of fusion with the mother and because of the realization that the mother must be shared with a third party, the father. This conundrum generates complex dynamics which structure the psyche: identifications, exclusions, new identifications with the parent of the same sex and with the one of the opposite sex alternate. These dynamics will culminate in adolescence, when we begin to see the recognition of one's own gender identity and of the difference between generations. Speaking of the Oedipal complex from a psychoanalytic perspective, therefore, means highlighting the internal, unbeknown, scenario of love and hate towards our parents. This perspective also focuses on our need to refer to two objects of love, our parents. They enable us to structure ourselves internally, to become the subject of our own history and to develop thinking abilities.

Omnipotence of thought and action   A defensive response to any sense of powerlessness which leads to the belief in the absolute power of one's phantasies, where internal and external reality are merged. In destructive omnipotence, the phantasy is so powerful that it is felt capable of causing damage in external reality.

Partial object   It is a particular aspect or function of the object attributed by the Self (e.g., the mother's breast as a source of nourishment). Relationships with partial objects characterize the schizoid-paranoid position. In the depressive position, different emotional experiences in relation to the object become more intergrated, in this way relationships are with 'whole objects' (e.g., the whole mother instead of part of her, her breast).

Pleasure principle   In Freudian theory, pleasure and displeasure constitute the basic regulatory principles of psychic life. The flow of psychic events is governed by the pleasure principle seeking immediate gratification of all needs, wants and urges. When these needs are not met, the result is anxiety or tension. For Freud the pleasure principle is what reduces the quantity and the intensity of excitation in the psychic apparatus.

Primary defences   Defensive processes present in every individual with the aim of defending against anxieties. Primary defences can interfere with the development of personality as they actively want to maintain physical and mental balance and protect from painful feelings that are a source of insecurity, danger, tension, or anxiety. Primary defences operate at an unconscious level, their functioning can distort or erase aspects of reality. When these defensive modalities are used excessively, they can hinder normal developmental processes.

Projection   A process that attempts to place the origin of conflicts outside the Self or to attribute them to others, who become depositaries of ideas, drives, affects and attitudes that the subject disowns. The infant projects its impulses of love and attributes them to the 'good breast' just as it projects out destructive impulses and attributes them to the 'bad breast'.

Projective identification   It is the opposite of introjective identification although the two mechanisms are complementary: in projective identification parts of the Self reside within an external object with which the Self then identifies. It is a very primitive unconscious process that operates from the earliest moments of life when the anxiety of separateness threatens the infant's integrity. This anxiety, which becomes intolerable, is denied by the infant and projected into the maternal mind, where it is contained and given back to the infant in a modified, more bearable version. In normal conditions projective identification determines an empathetic relationship between the infant and the mother: it allows, in fact, to put oneself in the other's place, better understand their feelings, contain and alleviate them. It can become pathological when it occurs frequently and intensely at other stages of development, with destructive and omnipotent characteristics (in this case, it is called intrusive identification).

Psychotic episode   An episode in which a temporary fracture with reality occurs; the latter is rejected in order to deny the source of one's internal suffering.

Psychic equivalence   A way of thinking in which what is happening inside our minds feels so real that it is equated to what is happening in real life. It is something that blocks our ability to relate to ourselves and others.

Psychotic functioning   Severely disturbed mental functioning, in which alterations of perception (hallucinations) and thought (delusions and fragmentation of thought connections) occur without the awareness of the subject. Contact with external reality is massively altered, compromising the ability to function and relate to others.

Puberty   It is the period of transition from childhood to adulthood in which numerous physical and psychological transformations take place, unfolding sequentially until the attainment of sexual maturity. The speed of these changes naturally causes a tremendous psychological upheaval requiring psychic work which integrates the development of the body. While the pre-pubertal child is passive, tender, and seduced, the pubertal child becomes active, potentially seductive, a source of passion. Puberty represents the moment of separation and distinction that puts the functioning of the Ego to the test as, at this juncture, the Ego must consider the needs of internal reality as well as those of external reality.

Reality principle   It is opposed to the pleasure principle. Initially, drives tend towards immediate discharge to fulfil desire; subsequently, through experiencing reality, one learns to achieve delayed gratification with more adaptive behaviour.

Regression   Involves a retreat into primitive forms of thought, action and sensation, repeating behaviours already held at a less mature age.

Repression   A defensive process by which an idea, causing pain, guilt, and anxiety, is excluded from consciousness. This process establishes itself in childhood due to the immaturity of the mental apparatus. Faced with situations that are too distressing, unbearable and unmanageable, the child can resort to an extreme form of repression, amnesia.

Resistance   A term referring to the patient's unconscious opposition to accessing deep internal dynamics. In the absence of ideas or thoughts, it is likely that there is a force at work which does not allow their expression; in this case the therapist explores the forms of resistance that intensify when the core pathogenic disturbance is approached.

Rêverie   A term used by the psychoanalyst Wilfred Bion to indicate the ultra-receptive mental state of the mother towards the communications of the newborn or of the therapist towards the patient. The process of rêverie allows the mother's mind to accept and understand the feelings of the newborn (hunger, fear, pain, etc.), thus making them tolerable. Through this experience, repeated in the mother-child relationship, the child acquires the ability to think.

Sadism   A term suggesting an extreme, pathological degree of aggression, specifically linked to sexuality. Sadism exacerbates the hidden cruelty which lies behind normal aggression, typical of human experience and behaviour.

Sadomasochistic relationship   It is a bond in which, as a genuine reciprocal relationship is possible, dynamics of power and omnipotence dominate. The use of pain prevails in the workings of attachment, defence, and gratification. The goal is the control of the other. Hostile feelings, aggressive, self-destructive behaviours and victimization cycles are repeated. The search for suffering and the attachment to pain used to maintain a bond with the other, stem from disturbances in the pleasure-pain economy in early mother-infant interactions, where sensations of pain and anger about having and not having prevail. These disturbances mark the beginning of a dependence on pain that can continue through other developmental stages.

Self-harm   Body-harming behaviours expressing both the adolescent's hatred, impossible to integrate, towards the new sexualized body and the aggression towards the parents. Self-harming behaviours should not be confused with behaviours marked by recognizable suicidal intentions. According to François Ladame, behind self-harming acts lies the fragility of adolescent narcissism that renders them intolerant to psychic suffering. Self-harm becomes an attempt to test one's own reality in relation to the external world, an effort to feel real.

Self-regulation   A method to master internal and external forces through the full use of one's mental and physical capacities, this enables to be efficacious and competent in the adaptation to reality. A fundamental need for homeostasis and control is at the core of a sense of self and self-esteem. One can structure an open system of self-regulation that allows tuning into reality with competence and creativity, or a closed system of self-regulation, which avoids reality and is characterized by power dynamics, omnipotence, and stagnation.

Schizoid-paranoid position   The concept of position differs from Freud's psychosexual stages of development. A 'position' suggests the fluidity or alternation of a psychic state. It provides a structure of affective life and an organization of the Ego regarding the relationships with objects, the nature of anxiety and the defences activated to control it. The ways in which the child overcomes the positions determine its future relationship with the external world. In particular, the schizoid-paranoid position is a mental state characterized by the splitting of objects into extremely good (ideal) or extremely bad ones. The Self relates to partial objects rather than whole and integrated ones. The concern is only with its own survival, not that of the object, whereas in the depressive position, there is also a concern for the survival of the good whole object.

Separation   In adolescence, it is the process that defines the distinction between the Self and the Other. This involves overcoming infantile ties, renouncing a grandiose representation of the Self, as well as renouncing parental figures, so far held as idealised oedipal objects. The process of separation enables the possibility of autonomy.

Sexual   In a psychoanalytic perspective, the sexual does not coincide with sexuality. If by 'sexuality' we mean the functions and physical excitations specific to the sexed body, by 'sexual' we refer more globally to the psychic functioning mobilized by what happens in the sexed body; and conversely, how the psychic aspect influences and conditions the body. In other words, satisfaction is not exhausted by the fulfilment of bodily needs but depends on the phantasies intrinsic in the relationship with the Other. This particular meaning of 'sexual' deals with the psychic dynamic of the subject and with its identity.

Skin experience in early relationships   According to Esther Bick, the most primitive aspects of the personality lack cohesive capacity and must be held together through the skin, which functions as a boundary. The initial state of disintegration in which the baby finds itself at the beginning of life, drives the need for a containing object (the mother's breast, a light, a voice, a smell, or another sensible object) which can be experienced by the baby as something that can hold it together. This containing object is concretely experienced as a skin. A defective development of this primary function of the skin can lead to the formation of a 'second skin', through which dependence on the object is replaced by pseudo-independence and by the inappropriate use of certain mental functions; this is done in order to create a substitute for the skin's containing function.

Splitting   A mechanism that plays an important role in the development of thought. It provides a psychic organization which operates by separating psychological representations based on their opposite qualities, thus allowing the Ego to emerge from chaos and to create some order in its experiences. Splitting becomes pathological when the separation occurs in very violent ways, preventing the integration of positive and negative characteristics.

Sublimation   A type of defence mechanism where socially unacceptable impulses are unconsciously transformed into socially acceptable behaviours.

Symbolization   An indirect or figurative representation of an unconscious idea. According to Freud, dreams or symptoms are the symbolic expression of a defensive conflict.

Therapeutic alliance   It represents the quality of the bond and the awareness of the collaborative tasks that hopefully can be established between the therapist and the parents, and between the therapist and the patient. It aims to promote the development of therapy, a development which doesn't have a predetermined path but proceeds in terms of depth and level of elaboration. A successful therapeutic alliance promotes the fine tuning of the relationship, offers a model of partnership beyond therapy and highlights the gratifications of reciprocity and of mature interdependence.

Transference   The concept of transference is a re-enactment and reactivation of past experiences. Feelings and thoughts experienced in a significant relationship of the past are transferred into the current relationship with the therapist. Transference is present in every interpersonal relationship, but it is a unique tool in the therapeutic relationship. Within such relationship, transference can be positive (characterized by esteem, affection, and consideration) or negative (characterized by envy, aggressiveness, and jealousy).

Transgenerational transmission   Transmission of negative experiences across different generations. These experiences were unfulfilled or they lacked psychic metabolization. Although such experiences might never have occurred in subsequent generations, they continue to mentally haunt as they were never previously explored properly. In this scenario what cannot be represented or thought about dominates.

Unconscious phantasy   It is a concept that has progressively expanded in psychoanalytic thinking. It refers to the primary content of unconscious mental processes. It is one of the cornerstones on which Klein's hypotheses about psychic life and its development revolve. Phantasies mainly concern the body and are the psychic representatives of instincts (libidinal and destructive). The earliest phantasies are experienced as sensations, later they become images that, with experience, can be verbalised. Phantasies (internal reality) interact with external reality, each has an effect on the other. They are an essential aspect of mental functioning.

Index

For Product Safety Concerns and Information please contact our EU
representative GPSR@taylorandfrancis.com
Taylor & Francis Verlag GmbH, Kaufingerstraße 24, 80331 München, Germany

9 7 8 1 0 3 2 3 9 7 4 7 4